PRAISE FOR *FOREVER ON POINTE*

"Honest, uplifting, funny, and generous, Agota Gabor's memoir captures a unique and enthusiastic woman whose life is an inspiring journey of hope and courage."
—The Right Honourable Adrienne Clarkson, Former Governor General of Canada

"I *loved* this book. It's simply amazing—what a roller-coaster life of highs and lows, triumph and tragedy. Agota Gabor is a fine writer."
—Charles Pachter, artist

"Inspiring and engaging! Although polio crushed her ballet dreams, Agota Gabor's steely determination made her reach for a high bar all her life. After she survived war and revolution in her Hungarian homeland and escaped to Canada, she reinvented herself several times in order to scale the heights of media and business."
—Lloyd Robertson, journalist, former news anchor at CBC and CTV television networks

FOREVER
on POINTE

FOREVER
on POINTE

A TRUE STORY

AGOTA
GABOR

glissade productions

Edited and designed by Girl Friday Productions
www.girlfridayproductions.com

Cover design: Anna Curtis
Project management: Laura Dailey and Reshma Kooner
Developmental editor: Shannon O'Neill
Image credits: All images courtesy of the author

ISBN (hardcover): 978-1-7779040-3-6
ISBN (paperback): 978-1-7779040-1-2
ISBN (e-book): 978-1-7779040-2-9

To my mom, Magda, my husband, Bill, my daughter,
Kathy, and my grandchildren, Carter and Lexi.
I love you so very much.

And to Koko, Brigitte, Margo, and Mary Lou—
the women who shared my journey.

Nothing is impossible; the word itself says "I'm possible."

—often attributed to Audrey Hepburn

CONTENTS

Ballet rats of the Budapest Opera House

CHAPTER 1

BALLET RATS

Ballet rats. That's what they used to call kids like me. If you visited a major opera house anywhere in the world, you'd find us: scurrying underfoot at rehearsals, loitering about during the off-hours, eagerly watching any event or performance. We ate, breathed, slept, dreamed, worked, and lived for the love of ballet. Study, sleep, practice, perform. That's all we did, and we loved it more than anything we could imagine.

Becoming a ballet rat is not easy. For starters, you must be the right age, height, and shape: preferably not too tall, with strong muscles and flexible joints. You need a perfect sense of rhythm and a relentless determination. You need stamina and perseverance. On top of all that, you must be able to express yourself through movement.

As a child I was a rat in the Budapest pack, at the opera's ballet school. It was incredibly hard work. But it also made for a magical childhood, one I wouldn't have traded for the world.

When I was almost eight years old, I decided to try out at the annual countrywide open audition to join the school. The audition was held in the large rehearsal hall of the Hungarian State Opera House—and good thing, because close to five thousand kids showed up every year. Only around thirty would be admitted. I hoped I would be one of the lucky ones.

It seemed ballet was in my blood. My aunts Klara and Kati were dancers. They had a sister act and traveled all over Europe before World War II. As a child I saw many pictures of them dressed in lovely costumes. They were beautiful, almost magical to me.

When they came home between engagements, I would ask them to show me steps, and sometimes they let me dance with them. They thought I was talented and had good rhythm, so they took me to a dance teacher when I was just over three years old.

A good ballet teacher can determine quickly if a child has true potential. All it takes is a few key movements, and a discerning viewer can see who has a future on stage. When I was seven and a half, my teacher suggested I try the audition.

The audition for the opera ballet school was not long.

There were five judges and one teacher. We were split into groups of sixteen and positioned into four lines. We were then shown some simple warm-up moves and told to do a few port de bras combinations. The jumps came next; we did them line by line. Turning exercises were last. We had to try to do pirouettes diagonally, from one corner of the rehearsal hall to the other. We had to do the chaîné turn: on tiptoe, or demi-pointe, you take a step diagonally to the right; as you bring your other leg in, you turn. In order to keep your balance, you must learn to spot, meaning you look at the corner of the room where you're aiming to go for as long as you can, then do a quick turn and look back at the same spot right away. This was easy for me because I was a natural "turner." We were then taught the reverence, a low curtsy performed at the end of every ballet class—a thank-you to the teacher and the pianist.

When it was my turn, I gave it my best and didn't fumble, and then went to wait with the other girls in a long hall. We were all anxious, trying to size each other up, wondering who would get in. I knew only one girl there, Koko, who would later become my best friend. After about an hour, the teacher came back and read out a list of names; those kids were told to stand to one side. "Agota Laczko," she called out, and I nervously ran to join the line that was forming. A few minutes later she stopped reading names, thanked the remaining children for coming, and sent them home. I had made it. I was officially a rat! So was Koko!

For those of us between the ages of seven and twelve, our days began when we arrived at 7:30 a.m. and made our way to the fourth floor of the opera house, to the kids' dressing room near the ballet rehearsal halls. The dressing room was our homeroom. It was not just a place to change; it was our safety zone. We spent a lot of time there during the day between classes and rehearsals, and at night during performances, waiting to go on stage. In some operas, like in Gounod's *Faust*, we appeared only in the first and last acts—that meant hours of waiting, playing, gossiping, and even sleeping in our dressing room.

On a normal day, our first class began at 8:00 a.m. Our morning ballet class lasted an hour and a half, six days a week. Daily class is the root of ballet. It is essential for learning and improving technique, but the purpose is not just repetition and training. With the time-honored progression from simple plié at the barre to complicated combinations with big jumps and turns, each class is also an ongoing audition. It is in this forum that you show your strengths and potential, how you relate to your classmates, and whether you have what it takes to be chosen for future parts. It is in *class* that a dancer's career is decided.

There is an order to who stands where at the barre. Your spot at the barre is your rank, according to how good you were the day before. Rats are very competitive; it's in their nature. Our ballet master, Ferencz Nádasi, was a famous dancer who was well known across Europe. He knew all about how competitive we were, and he thought this was as it should be.

As far as we were concerned, Master Nádasi was the King of Ballet. Our future was in his hands. He was a short, athletic man who wore a uniform of soft gray cashmere pants, a black T-shirt, and a gray wool vest or a gray sweater. He carried a stick, which he used to correct us. He would lift our leg a little higher with it, or he would gently push at our knee to straighten it. He was strict but not punishing. He motivated us by complimenting us liberally for what we did right and ignoring us if we failed. Every move counted. If your plié, battement, or arabesque was the best that day, you might be moved up at the barre the next day—and that move would escape no one's notice.

Classes were hard. One and a half hours doesn't sound like a lot, but when you are being pushed to your limit and you're eight years old, it can be quite exhausting. It hurt to hold a pose, and Master hurt us when he pushed our legs behind our ears and told us to stay that way. There was the physical pain, and then there was the fear. You were always afraid that the girl next to you would be better. You wanted to be the best.

The girl ahead of me at the barre was often my best friend, Koko. She was born in France; her parents lived there for a few years but came back to Hungary when she was a baby. She told me her mother didn't like France.

Koko and I were the best dancers in our class. We knew this from the attention we got from Master and because one of us was always picked to interpret the hand gestures Master gave, which were a sort of sign language for the combinations he wanted us to practice. For nondancers, these hand gestures might look like someone fidgeting or knitting without wool in the air, but to us they spelled out the various steps of a dance combination, which we then demonstrated for the rest of the class.

Koko and I were best friends and competitors. We both aimed for the stars. We were ambitious—I perhaps even more than she. Even though I couldn't help it, my drive to be the best sometimes bothered me, since I loved her.

We were as opposite as two kids could be. She was blonde, shy, and pretty as a doll. I was olive skinned and dark haired, with high cheekbones, hazel eyes, and a quick temper. She was better at jumps and I was better at turning. Her dream was to dance Maria in *The Fountain of Bakhchisarai*; I wanted to do the part of Zarema. We both dreamed of being the Odette/Odile in *Swan Lake*.

After our morning class we went on to rehearsals, where we children were taught our parts in various operas and ballets. Then we had lunch, which we brought from home and ate in our dressing room. At two o'clock we went to school.

Our schoolroom was a large dressing room on the fourth floor, one room for all grades. We were in school from two to five in the afternoons, six days a week. Our teacher was a large-bosomed lady, Mrs. Tuba, whom we all loved. She had a great laugh and never seemed to get mad.

We had little free time, and when we did, we loved to explore the House—and what adventures we had. The Hungarian State Opera House, as the Budapest Opera was then called, is a neo-Renaissance gem. Designed by Miklós Ybl, Hungary's greatest historicist architect, it was commissioned by Emperor Franz Joseph for the millennium celebrations in the nineteenth century. It is said that the emperor's directive was to make the opera house grand in every way, but to make sure that it was smaller than Vienna's. The emperor didn't want it to outshine the landmark of his hometown. Our opera house had statues of great composers, including Mozart and Beethoven, adorning the facade, and seated statues of Franz Liszt and Ferenc Erkel standing sentry at the main entrance. Next to them were imposing stone sphinxes that guarded the finely carved wooden doors. On the left was a carriageway and the entrance to the Royal Staircase, and on the right, on Hajó Street, was the artists' entrance.

When you approached the porter and he said hi, you knew you were special. You belonged. This was the entrance for those in the know. We were very proud as we walked into the building through this door every day. After we climbed the few steps leading inside the large building, the first thing we'd see was the orchestra pit on the left, and a little farther in we could glimpse the entrance to the stage. The opera singers' dressing rooms and the costume rooms were upstairs, on the second and third floors. The fourth floor belonged to the professional dancers and to us, the rats.

This building was our universe and our home. The rehearsal halls and dressing rooms were as familiar to us as our living rooms and bedrooms. The whole building was imbued with the smell of sweat and the sound of a multitude of pianos being played at once—sound pouring out from everywhere.

Exploring the fifth floor and above was not allowed, but of course we did it anyway—and oh, it was fun. The sets for seven different performances, both ballets and operas, were stored there at any one time. Walking among them on the thin rope walkways was dangerous, but it was one of our favorite pastimes; it was also good balancing practice! On nights when there wasn't a performance, we'd sneak out to the front of the house and play among the plush red chairs, each shining with seven kilograms of gold used as ornamentation. We'd pretend that phantoms and villains were hiding behind the huge crystal chandelier. Simply put, we were in heaven. Being a ballet rat was truly magical.

Of course, there was also a life outside the opera house. And in those days in Hungary, life was often very hard. It's no wonder that my mom and I stayed very close for the rest of her life. Circumstances helped to make it so. Mom was a warm and beautiful woman with lovely hands. I used to play with them every night as I went to sleep. She was very strong, and I believed she could do anything. She always told me that I could too.

I remember that when I was very little, maybe three, we had a German nanny. I called her Fraulein and spoke

only German with her. We lived in a large apartment just
off Andrássy Avenue: my parents; my brother, Ferenc, and I;
Fraulein; and a maid. My father was a successful businessman. He was in the import-export business, and he also
owned a canning factory in Nyiregyháza, a small town in
the north of Hungary. He had a lovely red Mercedes convertible, and my parents also owned a small house in a suburb of Budapest, where my grandparents and my mom's two
sisters lived. I remember visiting them on weekends and
being spoiled by Nana, whom I adored.

Then all that changed. My father left, my parents
divorced, and my brother was sent to boarding school in
Tata, a small town in the provinces. Not long after that, the
Germans occupied Hungary, the Nazi government took
over, and Mom, who was Jewish and had lost the protection
of my Catholic father, took me into hiding.

Some of my very first memories are from the siege of
Budapest, in 1944, which my mom and I survived together.
My grandparents and aunts were deported.

I was very young, but some of those memories I will
never forget.

I have a vivid recollection of traveling on a train with
Mom to visit my brother at school. Planes suddenly appeared
above us and started shooting at the train. The train stopped,
and all of us passengers ran out into the cornfields. Mom
pushed me onto the ground and lay on top of me, grinding
my face into the dirt, as the planes swooped low and kept on
shooting.

As quickly as they had arrived, the planes left, and we
got back on the train.

The worst memory I have of those times was when my
mother and I hid in the hospital for wounded soldiers that

was built into the rocks of the Citadel, in the Buda Hills. I was sick with diphtheria. While Mom was able to get me into the hospital, she had to sleep outside among the rocks while I was recovering. I was worried about her and felt scared being inside with the wounded men, who were crying and sometimes screaming with pain.

I also remember Mom getting us false papers and a new last name. We had moved into a small house in the suburbs, and she told me to pretend I was mute. I was not allowed to speak to anyone for weeks, to make sure I wouldn't mix up my name or any other details that would blow our cover. I remember we'd gotten a little white dog, and I used to take her into the bathroom with me and speak to her, since she was my only companion. Then one day she got loose and was hit by a train and died.

Through all this, the siege of Budapest continued. There was bombing every night and street fighting between the Russians and the defending German and Hungarian armies. On Christmas Eve of 1944, our house was hit. My mom squeezed me under the porcelain bathtub and told me not to move a muscle.

When she pulled me out, she decided to take a chance. We walked across the city to my aunt Ica's house to hide in her bunker. Miraculously, we made it there, and a few days later, after the Germans blew up all of Budapest's bridges in retreat, the Russians liberated my aunt's building. We survived.

It was the early spring of 1945. Budapest was totally destroyed. My mother and I went out in search of my brother and my father, who before the siege had lived in a villa up on Rose Hill, the loveliest part of Budapest. We walked through the streets and I gripped Mom's hand for dear life as we navigated amongst the dead bodies, piled up to my waist at times. We found both my father and brother alive, but I will never forget that walk.

Fear, paralyzing fear, is what I remember most from that year. I was too young to know the exact reasons, but I remember being scared of everything. I believe the memory of that fear stopped me from truly acknowledging my Jewish background later in life.

Throughout my life, when asked about my religion, I would always say, "My mother is Jewish." But I would never say that I myself was, despite knowing full well that if your mother is Jewish, you are Jewish too. I was brought up as a Catholic under a regime that discouraged religion, and I was never taught about the Jewish faith or its customs, but deep in my heart I always knew that the real reason I never identified as Jewish was because I never stopped being afraid.

Two of my aunts, my mom's younger sisters, miraculously survived and escaped from Auschwitz. They arrived home looking like skeletons. Budapest was in shambles; there was little food and no order. Mom had to take care of her sisters, me, and everything else, and while I don't remember how, she did it. I was too young to be of any help, my brother was back in boarding school, and my father was busy with his new life.

I tried to help once, and it didn't go too well. That day I was home alone in our apartment when a Gypsy woman (Roma), dressed in colorful red-and-purple clothes, knocked on the door and showed me two chickens. She said she'd give me the chickens if I'd let her take a few things from our apartment. Chickens were like gold in those days, since after the war we were always hungry. Mom was always going to the country with jewelry and clothes to exchange them for food. I let the Gypsy in, she took some things, and, sure as her word, she left the two chickens. For many years after that, whenever I heard Mom looking for things, she was muttering under her breath that the Gypsy must have taken it.

In the wake of the war, dancing in the magical world of the opera was like a salve for my mind and body. My first appearance on stage was in *The Tales of Hoffmann*. My part was that of an African slave serving the lead singer wine in a golden goblet. We didn't have black children in Budapest, so they painted us dark brown. After the show, we were dunked in a communal bathtub. Often the next morning in class, brown stains showed up on the kids who'd performed on the previous night.

My next part was in the ballet *Coppélia*. I was one of the village children in the first act. We waited backstage for our cue, and when we heard it we raced onto the stage and ran around, chasing one another.

At Christmas I had a part as an angel in the short ballet *The Legend of Joseph*. I also had various parts in *The Fairy Doll*, the other short ballet we appeared in on Christmas Day. I loved being on the stage. I loved my life. It was my world, and I lived for it.

At the end of 1949, when I was ten years old, things were changing again in our country. Hungary became the Hungarian People's Republic, also known as the Dictatorship of the Proletariat. Mátyás Rákosi, the general secretary of the Hungarian Communist Party, took over as president, but all major political and economic decisions were made in the Soviet Union.

In my home, the changes were for the worse.

My father, who still had his import-export business, was arrested and accused of deliberately keeping oranges and lemons, which he had managed to import from Italy, from the Hungarian people. He was tortured, convicted, and thrown in jail. After a few months he was released. In 1950, he escaped to Austria with his new wife, their two children, and my brother, and from there they went on to Canada. When we found out that they'd left the country, Mom and I felt even more on our own.

Mom and my aunt Kati had opened a small café called the Matróz, decorated as if it were a sailors' bar in Marseille. It was a fun and popular place. At night they had live music, and Kati brought her wiener dog, Bobby, to work. It was my second home. The Matróz provided my mom and my aunt a good living.

In 1950 the café was nationalized, meaning that two government officials walked in, took the keys, and told my mother that the place now belonged to the Hungarian people.

It was against the law to not have a job in Budapest. My mom quickly applied for and got a position as a ticket checker at the opera house.

Every night around two in the morning, we would hear cars driving in the otherwise quiet night. We feared these cars. They came to the city to pick up families and relocate them to the country. The government needed apartments in Budapest, so it took them from the so-called undesirables, meaning anyone who was not from the worker or peasant class.

Before the war we had a three-bedroom apartment. One room had been destroyed by bombs and was not usable. Mom was smart and had the two other rooms opened up into one, hoping that the government wouldn't give one of our bedrooms to another family and we could still escape relocation.

On nights when I was in a performance at the opera and finished late, my mom would come pick me up and we would walk home on Andrássy Ut, a wide, lovely avenue famed for its chestnut trees. On our way we would pass Number 60, a notorious building that was the headquarters for Hungary's feared AVO, the secret police. Now it is a museum called the "House of Terror." Number 60 was where political prisoners were taken to be interrogated and sometimes killed. Ironically, this was the same building where the Nazis tortured their prisoners before the war. I remember Mom always held on to me tightly as we passed, and we gave the building a wide berth.

Things were also changing inside my world of ballet. The Russian ballet had always been world famous, and the Soviets continued the tradition of demanding high respect for dancers. With this Soviet influence, athletes and artists became more important to the Hungarian regime, and suddenly we ballet students were valued and admired.

Our life at school became more organized. While we were still rehearsing and performing at the opera house, we were now students of the newly formed State Ballet Academy, with our own studios across the street from the opera house. Our ballet classes lasted two and a half hours in the morning, and after that we had folk dancing, historical dancing, character dance, jazz, and music appreciation.

Our academic schooling was also taken more seriously. Instead of three hours a day, we now had classes from one in the afternoon to six in the evening, six days a week. We also became "pioneers," members of the Communist children's organization, where we received many hours of political instruction at the weekly meetings. We learned a simplified version of Marxism, a lot about the history of the Soviet revolution and the lives of Lenin and Stalin, and a good deal about Chairman Mao.

The tightening of the political regime affected us kids as well. My brother, Ferenc, then nineteen and living in Canada, sent me a picture of the car he bought. It was a second-hand Chevrolet, his first car. I showed the picture proudly to my friends. The next day I was called to the school office and accused of spreading capitalist propaganda. I was suspended from the pioneer organization for six months and told that if I did anything like that again I would be kicked out of ballet school. Obviously, there was a spy reporting everything that went on at school.

In 1950 the famous choreographer of the Bolshoi and Kirov Ballets, a man named Vasili Vainonen, came to Budapest to stage *The Nutcracker*. For us, *The Nutcracker* was a huge event and presented great opportunities. There were parts for kids of all ages. At age seven or eight, you could be a mouse or a toy soldier. From seven to twelve, you could be a guest at the big Christmas party scene in the first act. At thirteen you could be a bat.

There were also four featured parts for children to be danced en pointe. One of them, the most coveted child part in *The Nutcracker*, is that of Klara. I was too old for that part. I was eleven, and Klara had to be seven or eight.

The other big parts were to dance the pas de trois in the third act. Two girls and one boy would be chosen.

Nine of us were taught the parts for tryouts. Róna Víktor, Ángyási Erzsébet, and I won the competition. Víktor went on to become an international star, partner to Margot Fonteyn, and lover of Rudolf Nureyev.

Two days before the premiere of *The Nutcracker*, I got sick with a high fever. Mom tried to keep me home, but I knew that if I didn't show up for the last rehearsals my role would be given to my understudy, my best friend, Koko.

When I arrived, I could see Koko was getting ready for the rehearsal. She saw me and said, "I knew you would show up unless you were dead." She was right. I hoped that our rehearsal master, Manci-neni, would let me dance the pas de trois in the third act but allow me to skip out on being a mouse in the second act.

"No such luck," she told me. If I was healthy enough to do one dance, I was healthy enough to do both. The rat costume was very warm, and we had to wear heavy humps on our backs to make us look like rodents. My fever shot up and I thought I would faint.

Somehow I managed to finish the rehearsal. After a night of medication and hot steam, my fever broke. By the day of the premiere I felt fine.

The premiere was one of the happiest and most exciting events of my childhood. In the pas de trois, we each had a solo as well as our dance together. Our names appeared in the posters and in the program. At the end of the show, the three of us went in front of the huge red velvet curtain on our own to take our bows.

I danced the pas de trois sixty-four times. Then I grew too tall and became a bat in the second act.

Over the years, my peers and I got more and more serious about ballet. We lived to dance. But during summer holidays, we also enjoyed spending our days on Margit Island. Margit Island sits in the middle of the Danube, the great river that is at its widest as it flows through Budapest. The island is a national park with no cars allowed, only bicycles. There are two swimming pool complexes: one where athletes and serious swimmers train, and the Palatinus, a green oasis of a water park, which we loved. We used to bike to the island in the mornings and stay till dinnertime. As well as numerous cold water pools and hot thermal spas, the Palatinus had a wave pool and also a large picnic area where our group hung out and practiced some of the lifts and difficult steps seen in Russian ballets.

The summer of 1954 seemed to fly by, and we were looking forward to the coming fall season, when we would start to take classes in pas de deux and learn the techniques needed to dance the classics. Come September, I'd be one step closer to *Swan Lake.*

At my first solo recital

In The Nutcracker

Mom and me at a May Day parade

Master Nádasi and our class at the barre, including (from right to left) Koko, me, Adél, and Margit, during the last year before I contracted polio

CHAPTER 2

POLIO

At the end of that summer, my uncle who worked for a magazine asked me if I wanted to make some money doing some modeling for a teen fashion supplement. I was thrilled to be asked. I had never done any modeling before, but being a dancer helped; I found the photo sessions easy, fun, and lucrative. One day we were shooting with two little girls and me dressed up as if for a tea party, and I started to have a headache. As the afternoon wore on, it became worse.

Mom picked me up and noticed that I was getting feverish and had difficulty walking. She took me to our friend Dr. Fabian, who had been my doctor since birth. He always had a very serious look about him, and this time, after a short exam, he sent us home, telling me to take an aspirin. We went back to our small bachelor apartment and I lay down on the sofa. I started to get bad stomach cramps. Mom made one of my favorite foods, lecsó—a stir-fry made with spicy Hungarian sausage; green, yellow, and red peppers; paprika; and onions. Mom hoped it would help or at least distract me. Then my aunt Ica, who lived around the corner, came over with cherry strudel, another favorite of mine. But nothing seemed to help.

I remember having a high fever that night, but far stranger was that my right thumb had started to tingle and then feel numb.

The next day, Dr. Fabian came to our house, where he examined me and gave us the diagnosis: infantile paralysis, also known as polio. It was the first time I'd heard about the polio epidemic, which apparently hit Budapest as well as most parts of the world every summer until the vaccine was discovered in 1955. In North America, the epidemic had created panic and parents were encouraged to send their kids to the country to avoid crowds. But the Hungarian government denied the existence of the epidemic. We learned later that the Palatinus swimming pool, where I spent most of my free time during the summer months, was a hot spot for the virus.

When Mom heard the diagnosis, she started crying. I was almost too sick by then to cry, and I didn't know enough about polio to truly understand what was happening to me.

In Budapest there was a separate hospital for infectious diseases. Back then they flew a huge black flag on top of the building. I remember being in the ambulance, approaching that building, and seeing that flag.

I was petrified. The next few days I spent in a fog. All I remember is opening my eyes to find various doctors watching me, asking me to move my legs and arms.

Once the poliovirus enters the body, it starts traveling, and wherever it stops, it creates paralysis. If it stays only a short while, it paralyzes only the muscles, and they may later revive. If the virus stays for too long, it kills the nerves connected to a limb or an organ, and that body part becomes paralyzed. If it reaches your lungs, it's very dangerous; the treatment at the time was to put you in an iron lung, a contraption that acted as a bellows to keep the lungs moving artificially. If the virus reaches your heart, you will likely die.

I remember not being able to move my right leg or my right thumb. Then at one point there was commotion and I woke up in a casket-like structure; this was the iron lung, but fortunately I wasn't in it very long. Then they took me to a ward, and I remember being given an enema. Then I slept for a long time.

When I woke up, I was in a large hospital ward with around ten other girls, and I overheard them talking. They were discussing polio and how afraid they were of living in a wheelchair.

"Living in a wheelchair?" I asked. "I am a dancer."

One girl started laughing at me. "You mean you *were* a dancer; now you'll be lucky if you can walk with a cane."

Furious, I threw the covers off the bed and tried to get up. I managed to swing my legs out of the bed, but when I tried to stand up, they wouldn't support me. I landed on the floor in a heap. Then, for the first time since this saga had begun about ten days before, I became hysterical. They placed me in isolation. I was given strong sedatives and I slept. When I was awake, I just cried. I didn't dare try to get up to see if my legs could support me; I was hoping for a miracle and wishing the whole episode was just a dream.

After days of isolation, pills, and sleep, a handsome young doctor came in and explained to me that the girl who told me I'd never dance again didn't know what she was talking about. He said that I had a good chance of dancing again; I just needed to work on my physiotherapy. The more I worked, the stronger I would get, he gently explained.

I started physiotherapy at the hospital. First I had water therapy for three weeks. Along with other patients, I was wheeled into a huge pool area and lifted into a hot-water pool. In the water, we could move a little better. We did exercises, and staff members stretched our muscles to keep them from locking. It was very painful. In the fourth week, when I started walking with crutches, I began to do sessions in the gym. My mom could only have window visits, waving at me from the other side of a pane of glass.

For two months I lived in the hospital, petrified and alone. At the end of two months, I could walk only with a walker, very slowly and painstakingly. The quadriceps and hamstrings in my right leg were still very weak. The discipline I'd learned as a dancer kicked in, and I worked twice as hard as the other girls. I was determined to get better. I was determined to beat the disease, to get my body back in shape and make it able to dance again.

Then finally the day came when they let me go home. Everyone in our apartment building knew I had polio, and all our neighbors came out into the courtyard to welcome me home. I will never forget it. I could walk, but getting up three flights of stairs to our apartment was very difficult. I had to hold on to the railings, with everyone watching while I struggled and cried. Instead of a welcoming party, it felt to me like a horrible public spectacle. It was too much to bear. In the aftermath, I had another emotional setback. I became suicidal. I didn't want a life in which I would need to crawl up stairs. I was a dancer. If I couldn't move and dance, why live at all?

My dear old doctor and friend, Dr. Fabian, came to see me. He held my hand and said, "Consider this whole experience like being lost in a forest. You knew you must get out, but you didn't know how. What would you do? You would start walking from one tree to the next, and then the next, until slowly you'd find a path. If it was the wrong path, you would stop and search for another. But slowly you would find your path, the one that would take you out of the forest. You have to do it one tree at the time. You need to do it tree by tree, step by step. It works—you'll see."

I have thought of those words many times since, as I have searched for and changed the path of my life.

Dr. Fazekas, the handsome doctor from the hospital, came to visit us often. He explained the two options I had for physiotherapy. One was to go to the traditional rehab hospital, which would help, but he wasn't sure it was the right path for me if what I most wanted was the chance to get back to ballet. The other option was the controversial Pető Institute.

Established in 1945 by Dr. András Pető, the institute now called the National Institute of Motor Therapy is internationally known and respected, but the methods used there are still somewhat controversial.

The main objective of the Pető Institute was to help children with cerebral palsy live independent lives. Pető soon broadened his goal to include helping all children with mobility problems originating from nerve issues. Pető was talked about like he was a miracle worker. Mom, Dr. Fabian, Dr. Fazekas, and I all agreed that's where I would go.

András Pető was a fearsome man. The first time I saw him he was sitting at the end of a cavernous room, on some kind of pedestal. He petrified all of us who had gathered for admission. He made me walk over to him with my walker. Then he took it away.

"Walk now," he said.

"I can't," I said.

He roared, "When I tell you to walk, you walk!"

So I did, a few steps, and then I held on to the wall. He brought a step stool over. He told me to step up.

I said, "I can't."

He roared, "I heard you wanted to do ballet. So step!"

I stepped up, my knee buckled, and I fell.

"With the other foot," he said. Now I tried with my good left foot. "Now give me a hand, and do it with your other foot again." I cried that my knee would buckle and break. He said, "Do you want to dance or not?" And it went on like that, on and on.

His method was to build muscles, willpower, and emotional toughness. He tried to teach us to ignore the pain. "No" was not an option, not an answer. The discipline I had learned at the ballet was nothing in comparison to what we did there. The man was an ogre, a sadist, and a genius.

I went to the institute for a year, six days a week, from 8:00 a.m. to 6:00 p.m. I hated it. A lot of the other kids were much worse off than I. When they fell, they were left on the floor; neither the staff nor the other patients were allowed to touch them. Some took hours trying to get up again. We were told that only by trying would our remaining muscles take over the work and compensate for our weakened limbs.

The days dragged on. I was exhausted. I never gave up and I worked very hard. But I was lonely and scared. My world was ballet, beauty, grace, and music. Our gym screamed of misery, sickness, and pain.

My mom tried to help keep my spirits up. I remember that when I got home on Tuesday nights, she would tell me that the week was almost over. "You see, darling, tonight we go to sleep, and Wednesday is the middle of the week, so you're halfway there. Then it is Thursday, and you only have two more days to go, and it will be Sunday—you don't have to go, and we will have a great schnitzel dinner and play cards."

Her logic was questionable, but afterward, whenever I had a difficult job or was going through a tough period of life, I always thought of her phrases, heard her voice and her optimism.

By the end of the year, I walked. My right leg was weaker than the left, but I learned to compensate. The only real paralysis was in my right thumb. The poliovirus had stayed there too long and killed the nerve.

Before I left the institute, Dr. Pető said to me, "You will have to keep up the fight to stay well. You will be able to have an active life, you may even dance, but not ballet. Not like before. You'll never be strong enough for that."

I didn't believe him. I was sure that if I just worked even harder, I would be able to get back to ballet.

The director of the ballet academy at that time was Gyorgy Lorinc. He was a mediocre dancer and a Communist, but, as I found out, he had great empathy for my situation. He arranged for me to join his classes. They were much less advanced than the ones I was in before my polio, but starting there would help me get stronger, and at least I would be back in the world I knew and loved. Another bright spot: I was allowed to finish high school at the academy.

That year was the toughest of my life. Dr. Pető was right. Ballet was much too hard on my body. I was no longer strong enough, and in ballet there's nowhere to hide. You need full muscle control and strength; you simply cannot compensate. I almost killed myself trying.

My feelings of desperation and shame drove me to compensate in other ways. I started binge-eating pastries after every class. I gained weight. This frightened me, but I couldn't stop eating, so I binged and then got sick and then ate again. I became bulimic. I didn't know that it was a sickness and I never told anyone about it for many, many years. I was disgusted with myself, but I couldn't stop it. I was lost. What was I if not a dancer? If I couldn't dance, what could I do? I felt I'd lost not only my strength, but also my identity.

When Mom went to work, I wandered the streets of Budapest and ate pastries. I got very sick again. Mom found a therapist, and with his help I started to think about my future, about what I wanted and what I was capable of. I never told him about my eating disorder; I was too ashamed. But he managed to turn my mind toward the future, and slowly I stopped binge eating and got better. I remembered Dr. Pető telling me that I would be able to dance, just that I wouldn't be strong enough for ballet. I wasn't ready to hear that when he first said it. But maybe now I was. I slowly came up with a plan B. I would become an actress in musical theater, which in Budapest at that time meant the operetta.

Operettas were and are very popular in Hungary. Imre Kálmán and Franz Lehár's melodies are famous worldwide. In these operettas there are always two couples leading the company: the prima donna and her love interest, always a tall, good-looking actor; and the soubrette, who is cute and funny, with her comedic male partner. The prima donna needs to be a singer and an actress, and the soubrette, a dancer and an actress. I figured maybe I could become a soubrette. Mom encouraged me to go for it, telling me I would make a great soubrette. As always, she said she just knew that I would be the best.

The Academy of Drama and Film in Budapest had an operetta department that offered a four-year program. It was very difficult to get in. Thirty out of thousands of applicants were accepted each year.

I felt getting into the academy was my only chance to stay in the rarefied world of artists. I simply couldn't imagine going to a regular college or university, even if I could get into one with my bourgeois background. The academy was my last chance. I had to get in.

Applicants had to go through three auditions. We needed to recite a poem and perform one song-and-dance routine from an operetta. I recited "Erlkönig" by Goethe and sang and danced the number "Give Me a Sweet Kiss" from the operetta *The Gay Hussars*.

I knew I would ace the dance part, even with my weakened legs. I was good enough in acting, but, while I could always deliver a song, I knew that I was not a naturally gifted singer. Luck was with me, and so were the years of dance training, and I passed the first audition.

There was a week between the first and second auditions. The teacher in charge partnered me with a boy named Gerzson to learn a song-and-dance duet for the second audition. Gerzson was tall and skinny with a big nose, and super talented. He was a natural comedian and a great mime. He later worked for Marcel Marceau's world-famous pantomime company in Paris. Gerzson was also a wonderful person to be with and to work with. We practiced together for a week and we passed. I was relieved, grateful, and nervous. We still had one more audition to go.

For the third audition there was a different panel of judges. Gerzson and I did the same number we had performed the week before, and we each had to recite the poems we had done at the first audition. While we had had to wait almost a whole day before we got the results of the first and second auditions, this time we had to wait only two hours to find out that we'd both been accepted.

Being accepted as a student at the academy meant I was back in my world. For the first time since being diagnosed with polio, I felt happy and hopeful again. Gerzson and I became best friends. We spent a lot of time together, mostly walking and talking by the bank of the Danube. We also swam across it, from Margit Island to the Pest side. Gerzson was very funny, and he would entertain me for hours.

He came with Mom and me for a short vacation at Lake Balaton. I guessed that he was hoping for a romance, and although I didn't feel that way about him, I loved him very much as a friend and we had some wonderful times.

I loved and still love Lake Balaton. We called it the Hungarian Sea, because you can't see the other side. (Later I found out that you could fit not only the lake, but the entire country of Hungary into one of the Great Lakes in North America.) Siófok, our favorite village on the shallow side of the lake, had small hotels and lots of rooms to rent in apartment hotels and in private homes. There were café houses, bars, an amusement park, and sailboats and kayaks to rent. What we loved most was the warm, shallow water to play and swim in. I thought it a summer paradise, and so did my mom. Gerzson fit in well with us. Later I found out that

Gerzson's infatuation with me was clear to Mom and she was hoping I would reciprocate. That didn't happen.

We started at the academy in September. We had wonderful teachers: some of the best stage actors in Hungary, as well as dancers and choreographers and voice coaches. We had classes in acting, dancing, and singing; learned pantomime and fencing; and studied historical drama and art. We also took Marxism and political geography.

In our first semester of acting class, we had to create a short solo mime piece. I did a simulation of my time with polio, when I was still in the hospital and didn't yet know I was paralyzed. In my piece I reenacted trying to get out of bed, with my legs buckling under me. It was a successful piece—my teacher liked it and I got a good mark—but remembering my total helplessness and despair made me upset all over again, and I had a hard time getting back into the routine of my new life.

Fortunately, we were also working on a one-act play by Ferenc Molnár, which was light and fun to do. I liked acting and the academy, which was at university level, so we got a well-rounded education. My favorite academic subjects were economics, political geography, and political science, which for us meant the Marxist-Leninist ideology. I admired and believed the theory, despite knowing that when put into practice, it turns into a dictatorship. At least it did for us in Hungary.

I had found a new beginning—a path out of the forest. I was happy again. Little did I know that in two months the Hungarian Revolution would once again change my life.

CHAPTER 3

THE GOOSE— OR HOW I LEFT HUNGARY

November 17, 1956, was a rainy but warmish day.

I was in the Old Town in Pest with Gerzson. Old Town, or the 5th arrondissement, is the ancient inner city of Pest. Some of its churches and buildings were built in the Middle Ages, and several mosques were left over from the 150-year Turkish occupation of Hungary. There are lovely old cafés and small parks adorned with statues of famous Hungarian generals and politicians. It was a favorite place for young people to meet and hang out. But that day we were depressed. And indeed, the atmosphere was depressing. The buildings were full of bullet holes and broken windows, and parked Russian tanks lined the streets. We could still hear distant gunshots, just a few.

The revolution was over. It was hard to believe that only three and a half weeks before, we'd thought the Communist regime would fall, the Russians would go home, and Hungary would be free. The short-lived revolution was started by students like us, but was squashed by political groups and the Russians.

Gerzson and I had been in class together at the academy on the morning of October 23, when it all started. Word spread in class and in the corridors that we should all join the students of other Budapest universities in a quiet march to show sympathy with Polish anti-communist reformers.

We met with hundreds of others at the corner of Rákóczi Avenue and József Boulevard at two o'clock. We waited there for a long time. There were rumors that permission for the march had been denied, then that it was on, then that it was off again. Finally, it was a go. We headed toward the Józef Bem statue, where student leaders pledged solidarity with the Polish demonstrators.

From there we moved toward Parliament Square. As we walked, the crowd grew from a few hundred students to thousands. Within a couple of hours, flags appeared—the red, white, and green of Hungary's flag, with a hole in the middle where the hammer and sickle used to be. The chant started with "Free Hungary!" and very quickly changed to "Russkies, go home!" The whole scene was exciting and surreal. I had only seen revolutions and protests in movies, and I had only marched with my school in May Day parades. Now we were shouting for political change.

By nine o'clock at night, there were two hundred thousand of us at Parliament Square. The chant was asking for

Imre Nagy, a progressive politician, to speak. He spoke, promising reforms, and then he asked us to peacefully go home. I wanted to stay, but I was also scared. I wondered where my mom was. I also had on high heels and my feet were killing me. So I decided to go home. Gerzson and thousands of others didn't. They headed to the radio station and surrounded it. The result was tear gas and then gunfire. Lots of people were injured, and some died.

That is how the bloody revolution, in which thousands were killed, began.

After a few days of fighting, some of the Russian soldiers stationed in Budapest sided with the uprising. It seemed that we had won. People poured out of their homes; it was like a street party.

Mom and I lived near Margit Boulevard. We walked out to the street and saw everyone kissing and hugging. It seemed unbelievable. I remember bumping into my cousin Zoli, who was ten years old. He was very excited, running down the street as fast as he could. I asked if he was in trouble—were the Russians chasing him? He said no, his mother found out he was in a demonstration. He kept running toward his house.

I went to the academy to meet Gerzson and find out if there was anything we could do. We were given leaflets to distribute with information about the uprising, explaining that Imre Nagy was our new prime minister.

The city was a war zone. Stores were closed and fights erupted outside; there were Russian tanks on the streets. On the square near the famous Hungarian Parliament Building we found a horrible scene, the dead bodies of AVO members, Hungary's hated secret police, hanging from lampposts. I saw that same scene in other parts of the city as well. In spite of the death and destruction, the atmosphere overall was hopeful.

Two days later we ran out of food, so I went to line up for bread. I'd been in line for about an hour when Russian soldiers started shooting at us. Those of us waiting tried to hide in an alleyway and lie down, but we stayed close by so we could get back in line as soon as the Russians left. Suddenly a middle-aged man grabbed me and shoved a rifle in my hand.

"Here, you, shoot that Russian—see him? You kids started this, so go shoot him."

I had never held a rifle before. The man propped it in my arms and put it into position. I saw a Russian soldier, a very young guy with light-blond hair, aiming at me. The man shouted, "Shoot!" I didn't, but the Russian boy did. He missed. I dropped the rifle and ran home.

At that time my mom was working as the manager of the cafeteria in a large government office. She had the keys to the office, and she knew there was food there. So Gerzson and I walked across the city to get to her office building. On our way, we had to duck into doorways so we wouldn't get shot. We quickly learned to tell which direction the shots were coming from.

Finally we reached Mom's office and got some salami, chocolate bars, wafers, and coffee. When we made it home, Mom celebrated by making plum brandy; we all had some, and I smoked my first cigarette.

In the middle of those weeks of fighting, I got a call from someone I had met the summer before.

We had met in a grocery store. He was trying to buy some fruit, speaking in French. I offered to translate and we walked out together, chatting. He had dark hair and black, dancing eyes. I guessed he was around thirty-five, and he was very good-looking. To me, speaking with him in French was exciting in itself. He told me he was a film director from Paris. He asked me out on a date, and I was thrilled. We spent quite a bit of time together that summer. He took me to a movie and a soccer game, and I developed a crush on him. Then he then offered me a part in his upcoming movie, a French-Hungarian coproduction titled *Heroes of My Dreams*. He said I would be perfect for the part of a young Hungarian spy and assistant to one of the heroes. He said I should change my name to Marika Gabor for the purposes of the film. I, of course, agreed. The movie was originally going to be shot in November, but the revolution put those plans on hold.

Daniel had come to town nonetheless. When he called, he said he was staying at the Grand Hotel on Margit Island and was leaving for Paris the next day. He invited me for dinner. He also said he could get me a Red Cross care package.

Crossing Margit Bridge was dangerous. The fighting there was fierce. But I had a tremendous crush on Daniel, and there was no way my mom could stop me. I hitched a ride on a motorcycle to the island.

On Margit Bridge we were caught in a crossfire. One of the tires of the motorcycle was shot out. We swerved and I screamed, but the driver managed to get it under control, and slowly we made it to the island.

Daniel was charming and sympathetic when I found him and told him all that I'd gone through to get there, and how tough life was otherwise. He ordered me a drink to help me calm down. Then we went to dinner in the hotel's elegant dining room. We ate frog legs, drank white wine, and later had sex. It was my first time. It all felt very dramatic and

exciting, almost as if I were acting out the part of the myste-
rious spy I was meant to play in his movie. I don't know if I
would have slept with him in normal times. But these were
traumatic and dramatic days. The evening became part of a
big adventure—and the care package he gave me certainly
was useful. Daniel drove me home in a taxi. I never saw him
again, and I never had frog legs again, either.

For the rest of that week, we still thought Hungary had a
chance for independence. Radio Budapest pleaded with the
Western powers to intervene. They didn't, and on November
4, a new column of tanks crossed the border from the east.
A week later they reached Budapest. The Hungarian military and the people put up a tremendous fight. Hundreds
were killed and thousands wounded.

The Russians crushed the revolution. It was over.

Hundreds of young people and others involved in the
fighting were deported to Siberia. Gerzson's older brother
was among them. Soviet tanks lined the streets. I had to walk
around one of them parked in front of our apartment building every time I left our house. I got to know the soldiers
in that tank. Russian was a compulsory subject in school,
so we all spoke it quite well. I found out that the soldiers
thought they were in Egypt to fight the imperialist powers
at the Suez Canal.

In the meantime, there was no food. People were flood-
ing out of Budapest. The year before, most of the mines
planted at the western borders to keep Hungarians and all
other citizens of Soviet-occupied Eastern Europe behind
the Iron Curtain had been dug up. However, with the Soviet
tanks and the army back in earnest, we knew that the mines
would be back again too. Rumor had it that it was now possible to get across in one piece if you had a guide to help you

cross the border, but soon that wouldn't be the case. Mom didn't want to leave. She had a job, a home, and a life. But I wanted to get out.

Once again, my path through the forest looked dark and unclear. I was lost and scared, with no idea of what was next for me. I had been doing well at the academy and thought that I could go on to become a good actress. But deep inside I knew that my true talent was for ballet, and I also knew I could never do that again.

In the Hungary of those years, to get into any school, to get ahead in any profession, you needed to have the right parents and to come from the right background.

Under the Socialist regime, schools first admitted people whose parents were workers, and then they admitted the sons and daughters of farmers. Next were children of teachers, engineers, and other professionals. My father was a businessman. He owned a factory. My background was bourgeois—not a good thing. Only kids from the aristocracy fared worse.

In ballet I had been good enough to get ahead, in spite of my background. But would I be good enough at acting to stay afloat? I was lucky to have gotten into the academy. We were lucky to have been able to hold on to our apartment in Pest and not be relocated to the country. I feared that I couldn't get ahead in that political system. The cards were stacked against me, and I wanted to leave.

All this went through my mind when we were thinking of leaving Hungary. I simply could not leave without my mom. I wouldn't leave without her. So in the end, we made a deal.

The company where Mom worked was giving a goose to each employee. There was a huge line, and my mom was standing near the end.

She said, "You'll see. I will get a goose. I will make you a great dinner and then you'll forget about leaving."

I looked at the line and said, "And if we don't get a goose, we'll leave?"

She agreed.

She did not get a goose. They ran out. I went back downtown and arranged for two spots on a truck that was leaving the next afternoon for a village near Győr, not far from the border. The next day Mom closed up our apartment. We went to her sister Klara's house to say goodbye and leave the keys. We had to leave everything behind. We took a few paintings to Klara's, but the rest went to the state. Looking back, I realize this episode must have been terribly difficult for Mom. She was fifty-two and had to leave her whole life behind. I, on the other hand, was excited. We took birth certificates and papers, some dry sausage and salami, and went to meet the truck. There were twenty of us in the open back of the truck. It was 120 kilometers to Győr and another fifty to the border.

The truck driver had relatives in a village near the border, and he said if everything went well, he would take us there and we could spend the evening at their house until it got dark. Then our guide would come get us there and take us across the border.

On the truck we had one scare, when we met a company of Russian soldiers. They asked where we were headed. We lied, saying we were seeing relatives in the countryside. The Russian soldiers were known to snatch young girls off the trucks, so we were very worried, but as they started to grab me and another girl, a bus carrying foreign journalists came by. Not wanting to create an incident, they let us go. Ironically, there was a Canadian journalist on that bus, Charles Wasserman, with whom I would work ten years later on a documentary in Romania.

When we got to the village, we were put up in a barn and were given food. Around eleven o'clock at night, the guide came and described how he was going to take us across the border. He told us it would be around seven to eight hours of walking, mostly through the forest. We would have to travel fast, as we needed to reach the Bridge at Andau, across the Austrian border, before daybreak.

We faced two primary dangers on our journey. One of them was stepping on a mine. The other was running into a Russian border guard who would either shoot or arrest us. Some refugees had been known to make a wrong turn and end up in Yugoslavia, where the unlucky ones had to stay in a camp for up to two years.

It was a long walk. My mom twisted her ankle toward the end and almost didn't make it. But with some help from the others, she limped along. We were among the last groups to cross the bridge at Andau. It was blown up the next day. After we crossed the bridge, there was another three kilometers to go in order to reach the village of Andau, but Mom couldn't do it. She could not go one step further. We sat on the side of the road. The others in our group promised to send someone to get us. Sure enough, they kept their word, and a horse and buggy came by to pick us up and take us to the village.

In Andau, it was pandemonium. There were hundreds of us refugees wandering around, tired, excited, and confused. This was November 19, and we were among the last wave of two hundred thousand Hungarians fleeing the country to escape. The people in the town were great, helpful and welcoming. The border between Hungary and Austria was set with explosive mines again a few days later.

From Andau they took us to the Eisenstaedt refugee camp. We could see the magnificent Esterhazy Palace not far away, and we found out that the refugee camp was created in the space where the military cadet academy used to be. In fact, Mom told me my dad trained there as a cadet.

There was food, but not much. Instead the Red Cross flights coming in were full of soap, toothpaste, and toothbrushes. We had been there for about three days when buses pulled into the camp. Each had a country's name on it: USA, Canada, France, Australia, Germany, and others. These were the countries that had opened their borders to us. We were told we needed to choose where we would like to go and then register on the appropriate bus, and they would do the paperwork.

I wanted to go to France. Paris was my dream; maybe I'd even find Daniel there. But Mom was definite about Canada. After all, my father and brother were there. So we registered to go to Canada. They told us there would be at least a month's wait until they sorted out the transportation.

I heard that some students my age were being allowed to stay in cottages in a small town nearby called Petronell. I told the organizers that my mom was an excellent cook and could help prepare meals, and they let us both go there.

A handsome boy my age sat next to us on the bus to Petronell. We started talking. He had gorgeous, soft-brown eyes that I almost got lost in. His name was Ferenc, he was with his friend Laci, and the three of us struck up a friendship.

Our place was a comfortable cottage with three rooms, which held five students plus my mom. One day the landowner came looking for a person called Count Nádasy. To my surprise, my friend Ferenc, with the lovely eyes, said, "That's me." The landlord knew Ferenc's family and invited him to the castle for dinner. Ferenc asked if he could bring his friends—and we all ended up there.

We had fun in Petronell, a beautiful place not far from Vienna. Mom's ankle still hurt, so she was resting, but the three of us friends explored the area. My father had wired us a hundred dollars, so we had some spending money. We went to a café and ordered Coca-Cola. We didn't have Coke in Hungary, and we thought it would be some wonderful cocktail. It was good, but certainly not the cocktail we expected.

We toured the Esterhazy Palace, and then we made it all the way to Vienna, where we went to tour the opera house and, after that, went to see *Du bist Musik*, a musical film starring Caterina Valente. At that moment I decided to name my future daughter Caterina.

We still had at least three weeks to wait until we could get a plane or ship to Canada. We went to the central camp every other day to check on transportation. Mom and I managed to get on the first plane to Montreal because of her twisted ankle and my negotiation skills. The following week, my friends got on a ship heading to Halifax. The day before our flight, Mom and I got a hotel room on Mariahilfer Strasse, in Vienna. We were going to have dinner and a Sacher torte.

But first I wanted to have a bath. We had to pay extra for that, and I wanted to enjoy it. I stayed in the hot water too long, I guess, because when I came out, I fainted. Ferenc came and helped me up, and as he carried me to our room, he kissed me. It was the most romantic kiss I'd ever had. Now I truly was in love. I gave him my father's address, and he said he would come to join us in Montreal.

The next day Mom and I boarded a Scandinavian Airlines flight to Canada.

CHAPTER 4

THE SUGAR PLUM FAIRY

I had been on an airplane only once before, when Gerzson and I flew from Miskolc to Budapest the summer before the revolution. It was a short, forty-five-minute flight; we did it just to see what it was like to fly, and we enjoyed it. The plane we boarded in Vienna on that cold December day in '56 was so much bigger. It was a special flight the airline SAS had organized for Hungarian refugees. Nervousness and anticipation hung thick in the air. Some people were very scared. Getting on a plane was a first for most of the passengers. Older people were prioritized; Mom and I got on only because of her twisted ankle. We soon found out that none of the passengers spoke English, and I was the only one who spoke French, so the flight attendant asked me to be the translator for the whole group. Shortly after takeoff, the attendant took me into the cockpit and introduced me to the pilot and the crew. It was so exciting; we were flying over the clouds, and they showed me all the instruments. I then went back to my seat and chatted with Mom and some of the people sitting nearby.

One oddly memorable detail is that I loved the milk they served us. I had only tasted skim milk before, the only kind we had at home. I loved the richness of this whole milk and the butter they served us. When not sleeping, I ate practically all through the flight. The weather turned as we were nearing Atlantic Canada, and it got very bumpy. A lot of people were scared and praying. The flight attendant asked me to tell everyone to relax, that we were not in danger. About a half hour later, the captain told me that the weather was too bad for us to land in Montreal, so we would be landing in Toronto. He asked me to tell everyone that accommodations would be made for us in Toronto. I delivered the message, but by this time the passengers were getting increasingly concerned. Would we have enough fuel? What would happen if we didn't? About an hour later I was called to the front again to be told we couldn't land in Toronto either, so we would try to land in Windsor. Now people were close to panic. Some told my mother to stop me from going up to the front. They said I was flirting with the pilot and distracting him. Then suddenly the weather changed in Toronto, and we were able to land there after all.

Ours was one of the first flights to bring Hungarian refugees to Canada. The news photographers asked me to touch the ground as I got off the plane, and the next day there was a front-page picture of me in the *Toronto Star*, hugging my brother—who tracked the flight and drove to meet it in Toronto—and then of me touching "the ground of freedom." After we landed, we were taken to a hotel for a medical exam and to stay the night.

The next day, a Hungarian man who had been living in Toronto since the end of the war took my mother and me and some others who arrived with us to Simpsons department store downtown. He had made arrangements for us to shop there after hours to make things easier. We had two department stores in Budapest, and I had seen a department store in Vienna when we were touring the city with Ferenc and Laci, but I had never been to a North American department store. It looked especially huge with just our small group of about twenty-five people milling about. It was both intimidating and magical. We could pick the clothes we liked, within reason—and warm things, since we were warned about the Canadian winters. I got a lovely white wool winter coat, black boots, a pair of jeans, and a black sweater.

Then, since we wanted to join my father, Mom and I got five dollars each and train tickets to Montreal.

My dad met us at the train station. He seemed happy to see us both, but he said he hardly recognized me—understandably, since I was a kid when he left Budapest. I was a little nervous but happy to see him. I never knew him well and didn't know what to expect. He was then working as a taxi driver, and he'd been living alone since his divorce from his second wife, Ilona. He gave us a ride into downtown Montreal.

Dad made arrangements with a friend to give us a bedroom in her house. It was on Drummond Street, between St. Catherine and Sherbrooke Streets, right in the heart of the city. Just a couple of blocks away was Stanley Street, home of all the European-style cafés.

Montreal is the largest city in Quebec Province. It is on an island in the Saint Lawrence River named after Mount Royal, the triple-peaked hill at its heart. A beautiful city, it has everything: mountains, the water, and cobblestoned French colonial Vieux Montreal, complete with the Gothic revival Notre-Dame Basilica at its center. In the mid-fifties the city was bustling, cosmopolitan, and exciting.

The main shopping area, St. Catherine Street, was covered in snow. With glittering stores and people speaking English, French, and various other languages, it was all so different and so vibrant. After the drabness of Communist Hungary, the lights and lively bustle were energizing. And the department stores! While I was accustomed to seeing empty shelves and long lines for anything that was available, here on display were heaps of clothing, an endless array of dazzling jewelry, and mountains of chocolates.

In the dictatorial system in which I grew up, most of us tried to get away with whatever we could. So one of those first days, I walked into Montreal's lovely Ogilvy department store, took a birthday card, and walked away, just to see if I could. Nobody came after me. I decided people were very naive to leave all that paradise unattended.

The room we rented was only a few blocks from the Rosemary Café, a Hungarian restaurant run by my father's then-girlfriend, "Aunt" Boros, who was middle-aged—and not pretty. She was nice to my mom but kind of ignored me. She had a good business and seemed to know everyone. The Rosemary seemed to be the hub of everything Hungarian: food, people, and gossip.

A week after I arrived in Montreal, Mrs. Boros gave me a job as a waitress at the Rosemary. My dad told me that

Canada had no culture so I might as well forget about dancing or acting and do something useful.

I don't think I was a terrible waitress, but perhaps I did enjoy talking to the customers a little too much. And as it turned out, the Rosemary, which was on Metcalfe Street, was only a block away from the famous Bellevue Casino, where all the major variety acts performed.

The Rosemary's clientele turned out to be Hungarians or people in show business: singers, dancers, magicians, acrobats, and musicians from New York City and all over Europe. Back in Hungary, we had a compulsory second language in school, Russian, but I also learned French as an elective language. At the Rosemary, I was able to put these lessons to good use and speak with these artists.

One day, with two soup bowls in hand (goulash soups, the house specialty), I overheard the Belgian comedian I was about to serve saying something very funny. We all laughed, I leaned the wrong way, and the soup ended up all over him and his girlfriend.

Mrs. Boros was there in a minute, reprimanding me with a *You're fired* look. I started to cry as I cleaned up, and then I lost it. I told the Belgian guy how unfair life was. I told him what my father said about Canada having no culture, how it made no sense for me to dance or act now that I had landed in Canada, and how hopeless my future seemed.

He asked what kind of dancing I did. I told him every kind, that I knew jazz, modern, and character dance. He suggested I get an agent. Did I have any headshots?

The only photographs my mother had brought with her from Budapest were of me and my brother when we were kids. They were great studio shots, taken by a well-known photographer by the name of Varady.

Since thousands of Hungarian refugees ended up in Montreal, it was both surprising and not surprising at all that a few days later Mr. Varady, the photographer, walked into the Rosemary. Once I found out he was there, I went over to talk to him and offer him a deal I hoped he wouldn't refuse.

"Mr. Varady," I said, "I am sure you will start a photography studio in Montreal, and I am sure you will need to show some photographs you have taken. In Canada you will need a portfolio, I assume."

I persisted. I told him I hoped to dance in Montreal and needed photos: a headshot and a dance shot. He could use them for his Canadian portfolio. He agreed.

I was thrilled. Now, what to wear? My mom and her friend helped me put together a little ballet outfit—not quite a tutu, but it had to do. I also got some fake flowers, and I bought a pair of used toe shoes.

We then needed a location for a photo shoot. It was early March and very cold. Mr. Varady chose the rooftop of an office building where he was friendly with the assistant janitor, who gave us access. I'm lucky I didn't get pneumonia, because we worked on the rooftop for two hours, but the shots were great.

I sought out my Belgian friend from the fortuitous soup spill. He took the photos to his agent, who called and gave me an appointment for the following week. I could hardly believe my ears. I made him repeat the appointment time several times in case I misunderstood. My French was pretty good, but not fluent. I had heard him correctly. This was very exciting news.

My friend also told me that a dance number in a nightclub had to last at least five minutes. When I protested that

the most difficult solo in *Swan Lake* was only three minutes long, he told me nobody would hire me with such a
short number. If I couldn't dance that long, he said, maybe I
should sing a little.

There was only one dance number I remembered that
was almost four minutes long. It was Boccherini's Minuet,
which I had danced at a recital in Budapest.

I bought the sheet music for the piece, as well as
for Brahms's 5th; I thought a little czardas, the famous
Hungarian folk dance, would do for the second number.

The day came for my appointment. The agent asked me
about the dance numbers I would perform, and I tried my
best with answers. I guess I did well enough, because he gave
me a contract on the spot. It was for a weekend and two one-
week runs. All the venues would be medium-sized supper
clubs. On Friday and Saturday nights, I'd do two shows a
night in Valleyfield, Quebec. Then the show would move to
Rouyn on Sunday, run for a week there, and then go on to
Val-d'Or for another week.

I received $125 for the weekend and $150 a week for each
of the following two weeks. As a waitress, I was making forty
dollars a week, including tips, and that was if it was busy.

Mom was a little uneasy about my dancing in a nightclub, but since she was going to come with me and we
needed the money, she said OK. So in a couple of weeks we
were off on the bus to Valleyfield.

Valleyfield is a mining town two and a half hours from
Montreal. We arrived around noon, and after settling into
the hotel, which was next door to the club, we had a chance
to walk around. There wasn't much to see. We walked down
Main Street and saw the Chinese-Canadian restaurant, the
church, and the bank—the last two were by far the largest

buildings in town. Then, since it was a cold day, we went back to our hotel.

Rehearsal was to be at 5:00 p.m., and the two shows would run at 8:00 and 11:00 p.m. A singer was the master of ceremonies for the shows, and she also did the opening number. I was next, and the featured performer that weekend was a magician from Montreal who worked with pigeons.

At a quarter to five, Mom and I walked over to the club. It was medium-sized, with a small stage. I walked around the stage and found it slippery. I worried about the en pointe work I planned to do in my dance number. Since my polio, as much as I still loved dancing, I was always careful and afraid. *What if I fall? What if I get a cramp?* These thoughts followed me everywhere.

Then the band came in. We introduced ourselves and they started tuning up. After their warm-up, I walked over to the leader with my sheet music for Boccherini's Minuet. I apologized that I only had the score for piano, hoping it would suffice since it was such a well-known piece. He looked at me and then the score. With a smile he said, "Baby, we don't read."

I was a bit confused, but Mom came over and said that maybe if she played it for them, they could pick it up by ear. She played it, but they told us they didn't do classical and suggested that Mom accompany me on piano for the shows.

So we did just that.

Soon it was showtime. The place was full of men and gray with smoke. It was very noisy and I was very scared.

But, as they say, the show must go on. Mom walked to the piano and I onto the stage. It was still very noisy, so we waited a little. Then I walked to center stage, did a curtsy, smiled, and gave a nod to Mom to begin.

I think the club's audience was more used to belly dancers than ballet dancers. They seemed surprised to see me in my blue-and-white tutu, dancing to the soft sounds of a minuet.

The audience became shockingly quiet. As I was doing my final pirouette, I heard a booming voice yell, "My, my, if it isn't the Sugar Plum Fairy."

When I finished, there was laughter and whistling. Mom and I smiled as the men politely stepped aside for us to walk out. I thanked my lucky stars that the performance was over.

Walking back to the hotel, I realized that if I was to have a career as a nightclub performer in Canada, I needed to radically change my act. On our way to Rouyn, we bought the music for "Mademoiselle de Paris" and "C'est Magnifique," and we were off on our nightclub tour of Quebec.

Mom and I lived like vagabonds for about six months, traveling around Quebec, staying in small hotels, doing two shows a night. Mom stood at the side of the stage, never letting me out of her sight. It was hard work, but it was fun and a great experience. In Sorel, I was the opening act for the Everly Brothers. They were young too, and we became friends.

Crisscrossing the province was not without its humorous incidents.

Mom didn't speak English at all. She was trying to learn, but it isn't easy to pick up a new language in middle age. One of our bookings was at a big club in the Gatineau Hills, near Ottawa. I got a brand-new dress for the occasion. It was packed carefully in a white box with a ribbon.

We went by train from Montreal, and when we got off, I left my dress behind. Telling Mom to stay on the platform, I went back to get the dress. When I came back, I saw a big commotion and saw Mom standing in front of the train, in the middle of the crowd, waving her arms and shouting in Hungarian, "This train is not going anywhere. My daughter is on it!" They were trying to tell her that the train was not going anywhere at all for the rest of the day. But since she couldn't understand a word, she only calmed down when she saw me and my dress. Mom was embarrassed, but after that we just laughed. "The day Magda stopped the train" became one of our favorite stories.

That summer I received an unexpected gift from my father: a first-class train ticket to Niagara Falls, to visit my brother, Ferenc, who was now called Frank. I had a compartment of my own, and in the evening a wonderful porter came in and made my bed. I was so impressed, and felt as if I were in a movie—this was the North America of my childhood dreams.

Frank took me to see the falls, and we drove around town, where it seemed most women walked around with large curlers in their hair.

We also drove to Stratford, Ontario, to see *Hamlet* at the Stratford Festival. The performance was still held under the famous big tent, and I almost jumped out of my seat when the trumpets announced the beginning of the performance. Frank's car didn't have air conditioning, and on the long, hot drive back to the falls, he introduced me to soft ice cream. I loved it—so much that we stopped eight times to buy more.

I also loved spending time with my brother, whom I hadn't seen for a very long time. In fact, we had never spent much time together, since he had gone to boarding school when I was very young, and soon after that he left Hungary. Now he was all grown up and seemed totally North American. When I saw a big line snaking down one of the streets in Niagara Falls, I asked him if they were lining up for food. He laughed and told me it was a line to see a movie. Frank was excited about getting his green card and was looking to move to the United States. He was working for General Electric at the time, in their computer department.

One day back in Montreal, my Belgian friend told me he had heard of an opening for a dancer at the Bellevue Casino, which in the fifties was considered Canada's biggest tourist nightclub, with seating capacity for seven hundred. There were many nightclubs in Montreal in the late fifties, but the two big cabarets were the Chez Parée, on Stanley Street, and the Bellevue Casino, on Ontario Street at the corner of Rue de Bleury.

At the time, Montreal was one of North America's three most important "show towns," following Chicago and New York City.

I rushed to the Bellevue that afternoon. I auditioned the next day and, to my delight, I was hired.

The Bellevue was like a twin sister to New York's Copacabana; it featured international headliners—Dean Martin, Édith Piaf, Charles Aznavour, Jimmy Durante—and it hosted elaborate productions with beautiful showgirls, singers, dancers, and a sixteen-piece house band.

The producer that year was David Bines, a Russian impresario then living in New York. His wife, a former Ziegfeld girl from the thirties, was the choreographer. Later, in 1974, they brought the Bolshoi Ballet, with Maya Plisetskaya and Mikhail Baryshnikov, to Toronto for a tour. Baryshnikov defected from the Soviet Union while performing there, and, as it turned out, I would cover that performance as the entertainment reporter for CBC Television.

The shows produced at the Bellevue changed every month, with the headliners changing weekly. The production I joined was Gershwin's *An American in Paris*. I was in heaven. I was also scared. My recovery from polio was amazing, but not complete. When I danced, I had to constantly compensate for my weak right leg. My technique was good enough that I could fake most steps, but not each and every one. I lived in constant fear that my weakness would be found out and I would be let go.

With my contract for twelve months' work, Mom and I could rent an apartment on Metcalfe Street next door to the Rosemary Café. Now we had a home. I took some classes with les Grands Ballets Canadiens de Montréal, but only a few. They were challenging with my weak leg, and I couldn't keep up. The old pain came back. In my head I knew exactly what to do, but my muscles couldn't do it. I left the classes in tears, and soon afterward I stopped trying to do ballet. I decided I wanted to get into TV, and I started leaving pictures and résumés at Radio-Canada, CBC's French network, which was on Dorchester Street, near our apartment. It was a busy French-language studio and office complex where drama and variety shows were produced. I did get some small walk-on parts, which I loved to do and had time to do, since most of my days were free.

I enjoyed my life and enjoyed working at the Bellevue Casino. The dancers were mostly French Canadian and the showgirls mostly from New York City. I was amazed at the diversity of the dancers. There were a couple of French Canadian girls who were very young and very religious. They would come off stage dressed in beautiful, sexy, sequined outfits and head to the corner of the dressing room to kneel down and pray. There was also a lovely girl from Spain who always had two strong Pernods: one before we went on stage and one after the show, before she met her boyfriend. She said she needed Pernod for courage. Some of the showgirls were sophisticated and some were pretty rough characters. We did two shows a night, and the last two weeks of every month we rehearsed every afternoon for the next production. After the show we would go to Bens, the famous delicatessen at the corner of Metcalfe Street and Maisonneuve, and hang out there with all the other performers till four in the morning. My pay was seventy-five dollars a week, and Mom and I could make ends meet.

My relationship with my mom was changing now that I was nineteen and I was making the money. In some ways we couldn't relate the way we used to. Mom was a beautiful woman but not a happy person. She came from a poor Jewish family and was the second of four girls. Her dream was to become a concert pianist, but she married my father young, and he discouraged her from doing anything but helping him with his business and taking care of family life. Even so, she soon became an important part of his import-export business and helped him make a lot of money. They had a few good years, traveling to Vienna, Venice, and Paris during the peaceful years of Europe between the two world wars. Sadly, he fell in love with his secretary and left my mom, my brother, and me during the war, and forced my mom to agree to send my brother to boarding school.

After that it had been just Mom and me for most of my life. Now that I was the breadwinner, she became less like a mother and I less like a daughter: we were more like partners. I had talked her into leaving Hungary, and she had a difficult time learning English or French. She also found it hard to make new friends. I felt responsible for her and wanted to look after her.

One night between shows at the Bellevue, I was asked to join a birthday party. That was part of our job, to be beautiful and pleasant with the club's big spenders. The birthday boy was a man in his forties. His name was Arthur MacDonald. When I said, "Happy birthday," we all had a zombie, a very strong cocktail made of rum. I drank it much too fast, and I got sick when I went backstage. I wish I had recognized that as a bad omen.

The next night I received two dozen red roses and a gold necklace in my dressing room. It came with a note asking me to have a drink after the show. Arthur MacDonald was sophisticated and had a lot of money, and I was impressed. Over time, I learned that my sophisticated friend was also involved in the Mafia. I was petrified, and so was Mom.

Then at the end of 1959, the Chez Parée was blown up by a Mafia-like gang. Many people were injured, and Jean Drapeau, Montreal's mayor at the time, became serious about cleaning up the city.

The Bellevue Casino was closed.

Mom decided to spend some time with my brother, Frank, in Schenectady, New York. I was desperate to leave Montreal behind, and so I moved to Ottawa, where a friend told me of a job opening at the Arthur Murray Dance Studio on Sparks Street. They offered me training in teaching ballroom dancing and also in sales. It was the best and only sales training I ever had. I was thankful for it later, when I ran businesses of my own.

We were taught how to sell the introductory courses, when and how to sell an extra course, how to sell a lifestyle, and how to overcome customer objections.

With my background, I found the dance part of it easy and fun. I was a quick learner, and within a couple of months was able to teach Bronze, Silver, and even some Gold steps. Arthur Murray's method was detailed and well organized.

For each ballroom dance (waltz, foxtrot, swing, quick-step) and each Latin dance (cha-cha, samba, mambo, salsa), there was an exact number of steps for beginner (Bronze); intermediate (Silver); and advanced (Gold). Each student had a chart, and at each lesson we marked off what they learned. We always did school steps first, which students had to dance by themselves. After that we danced together. We worked on the steps, and we practiced leading and fol-lowing. I enjoyed many of the clients: young men trying to impress a date; couples; lonely older men and women. And then there were those who just loved to dance.

I became a good instructor. Most days I taught from 2:00 until 6:00 p.m., took an hour break for dinner, and then taught again from 7:00 to 11:00. I also became very good at selling. It had to be subtle. When a student's course was nearing its end, I would make myself heavy and difficult to lead, and then when we sat down to discuss his progress and plans for more lessons, I would remind him how much work he needed in order to learn how to lead.

I once sold a ninety-year-old man a lifetime course for thousands of dollars. I received a big commission and felt a little bad about it, but then again, he did sign the contract!

At Arthur Murray I met Brigitte, a German Romanian Canadian girl, who became my lifelong friend. She was eigh-teen at that time, blonde and beautiful. We became friends almost the first day we met. Brigitte still lived at home, and I used to have sleepovers at her house. I'll never forget her mom waking us up with espresso and plum snups on the side.

Brigitte and I used to double-date; we were busy with our social lives and had fun. I was dating the quarterback of the Ottawa Rough Riders football team. He got us some great tickets to the Grey Cup, but it was terribly cold that day.

Then my friend Arthur, from Montreal, showed up in Ottawa. He wanted to take me out again, and when I said no, he had me followed wherever I went. He sent me flowers and jewelry and never left me alone. For my twenty-first birthday, he sent me a red Fiat convertible. I didn't have a license and didn't know how to drive.

I knew if I kept the car, I would never rid myself of him. I was scared of him, but mostly I was scared of his friends.

Brigitte and I drove the car into a park and then into a tree. We were careful not to hurt the car or ourselves too much. I left a note in the car saying it belonged to Arthur, but I knew that having done that, I had to get out of Ottawa. Brigitte also wanted to leave her parents' house.

The next day, we took the overnight train to Toronto.

The Bellevue Casino's dance troupe

*My first publicity shot,
taken on the rooftop*

Top: My publicity shots
Bottom: Me, eighteen
years old

CHAPTER 5

TORONTO THE GOOD—TO ME

Toronto is a lovely city on the shore of Lake Ontario. In 1960 it had a population of 1.5 million people and it was still "Toronto the Good." There were no movies or shopping on Sundays, and during the week you couldn't get a drink past midnight. People dressed conservatively. There were no cafés. It was a far cry from vibrant Montreal. All my Montreal friends told me I would be bored sick in Toronto, but it ended up being a lucky place for me.

When I came to Toronto, many people regarded me as an outsider and some even as a "displaced person." But the city was changing quickly, and as a European immigrant I found it exciting to be part of the change. Italian and Hungarian coffeehouses started popping up in Midtown, and the Yorkville area filled up with jazz clubs and hippies. It certainly didn't yet compare to Montreal, which, until Las Vegas surpassed it, had been called the Sin City of North America, but Toronto never wanted to compete for that name. Toronto grew rapidly, and by the 1990s it had become Canada's economic center, and by the year 2000 it was one of the most diverse and cosmopolitan cities in North America, second only to New York.

When we arrived in Toronto, Brigitte and I found a bachelor apartment in Midtown on Rosedale Valley Road, close to the subway and with a balcony. The rent was $110 per month, which we hoped we could afford if we both found jobs.

We went to the Honey Dew coffee shop to check out the classified ads in the paper. There were several ads looking for house models for manufacturers on Spadina Avenue, Toronto's garment district. Brigitte found an ad for a size 10 model at Sporting Life, and I found a job as a size 9 at Klever Klad. At the time, house models helped out in the office at the switchboard as well as modeling the house lines for the buyers. The pay was sixty dollars a week.

We looked forward to furnishing our apartment once we got our paychecks. Living on our own was a first for both of us.

We bought one bed, a table and two chairs, and a chest of drawers. We separated the mattress from the bed to make two beds. We alternated sleeping on the more comfortable mattress, switching every week. We were on a very tight budget, living mostly on apples and hard-boiled eggs.

Our role model in those years was Holly Golightly from *Breakfast at Tiffany's*, minus her money and the cat. When we were taken out to dinner, our dates were always surprised by how much we could eat. Little did they know that we practically survived on those suppers.

Then we got a dog. We were looking to get a small dog, but when we looked at the rescues we fell in love with a very small German shepherd puppy that looked very sad and adorable. We just couldn't leave him. I always had and still do occasionally have trouble pronouncing the *th* sound, so we called him TH, reasoning that I would practice making the sound each time I called him.

TH grew quickly and soon became a gorgeous, lean, powerful dog with pointed ears and sharp teeth. Brigitte and I handled him like a baby, and he believed that he was one. When we came home from work, he would take one of our arms into his powerful mouth and make us run around our apartment at least five times. He held it between his teeth gently but firmly, so there was no way we could free it until he was finished with his greeting.

One day I got a call from the superintendent of our apartment building telling me to come home right away. TH had gotten out of our apartment somehow and was running amok in the building. I rushed home, but when I got there TH ran out of the building and onto the street. I ran around the neighborhood and eventually found my lovely big baby happily splashing around in a park fountain nearby. I was so happy to find him, but we received an ultimatum from the apartment office that we had to get rid of the dog or we would have to move. We were terribly upset. We couldn't afford to move and Brigitte didn't want to, and she couldn't afford to pay the rent alone.

Fortunately, a friend of ours had a friend who lived on a big farm and agreed to take TH. The farm was a beautiful place about an hour from Toronto, near Milton, Ontario.

The owners were a Hungarian couple who lived in a large house and had a German shepherd themselves, a huge dog called King. He was very friendly, and the two dogs seemed to get along. The owners were very nice and told us they loved dogs and would take good care of our baby.

We visited TH as often as we could get a lift, since neither Brigitte nor I had a car at the time. One day I called Iren, the lady who lived on the farm, to say I was coming for a visit. She said, "Please don't come, TH is not here." Then she started to cry and told me that TH and King had gone after a calf and killed it. Animal control put them both down.

I was shocked. My baby had been killed. I was sure it was King's fault (I still am), but there was nothing I could do. Brigitte and I just cried. With TH gone I felt alone and started to miss my mom and my family back home. But Mom seemed to be happy living with my brother in Schenectady. At the time, he had a small plane, a Cessna Skyhawk. Frank had started flying gliders at age fourteen, and he was a good pilot. He took Mom flying a lot, which she loved.

Life went on. I got used to working on "the Avenue." Spadina Avenue was bustling with models, buyers, cutters, and designers. Most of us were recent immigrants from Europe, and we made lots of friends. When not modeling Klever Klad designs to buyers in the showroom, I helped out at the switchboard and in the office. Brigitte and I started to feel at home in the city.

One night Frank called and asked if I would like to come for a visit. He would come and pick me up in his plane. I got a few days off from work, and he picked me up at the Toronto Island Airport. It was a great trip, especially flying low over Niagara Falls. Frank was still working for GE, now at their huge plant in Schenectady. He was renting a small bungalow in the suburbs. It was a cute and comfortable place, and I was so very happy to see Mom. I spent five days with the two of them. The trip was my first look at small-town America, which was very different from the big cities I was used to.

It was in Schenectady that I saw my first computer. Frank took me to his office, where the computer took up a whole wall, and he told me to ask it a question. I asked, "Do you love me?" The computer answered, "I am not programmed to answer that."

But the story I will never forget from that trip was Mom's adventure at the grocery store. Frank and I were at home when Magda rushed in, very upset. She said Americans were crazy, just like in the Westerns with their guns. How can people live here, she asked, with people pointing guns at a woman doing her grocery shopping?

She told us she was coming out of the grocery store with a few bags, when a man in uniform walked up to her and said something she didn't understand. The man repeated it, she still didn't understand, and she tried to push by him to get on her way. When she wouldn't stop, the man pulled a gun and pointed it at her. She told us she dropped her bags and put her hands up high. Then she said that she just stood there as a large, dark-brown truck pulled away. It stopped a little way down the street, and the same uniformed man came back to her, picked up her bags and handed them to her, said "sorry," and got back onto the truck.

We couldn't quite figure it out, so we asked her to come back with us to the grocery store. As we soon saw, next to the grocery store was a bank, and the truck was a Brink's truck waiting for a money transfer. The uniformed man was a security guard; he had been asking Mom to wait until the truck left. She insisted on walking toward the truck anyway.

Thus the incident with the gun. This became a much-repeated family story.

Not long after my trip to Schenectady, I was at work, being fitted for a dress, when I was called to the phone. It was Mom. She told me that my father had died the night before. I was shocked, not only by the news but also by how I felt.

I felt sad, but I didn't feel grief the way I thought I should. I had very few memories of him, and most of them were negative.

I clearly remembered that in Budapest during the war, he didn't help Mom and me when we were hiding from the Nazis. When we were starving and went to ask him for food, he said, "One should stretch only as long as the blanket cover." I remember that strange saying because Mom repeated it many times. I knew it meant that he'd turned us away.

When Mom and I first arrived in Montreal, I had one nice dinner with him, but he didn't offer much in the way of help. A couple years later he tried to get Mom to go back to him, but she couldn't forget the past and refused.

We learned that he had had a heart attack and was taken to a French-speaking hospital in Laval. When they asked him for the phone number of his next of kin, he gave them Frank's phone number in French, with one digit wrong. The hospital called the number, telling the person who answered that Frank Laczko was in critical condition. The person managed to contact my brother, Frank, the next morning, but by then my father was dead.

He was sixty-three years old. He had been a successful man in Europe, but he had a hard time finding his footing in Canada. He started a small wafer factory there, but before long he got ulcers and was hospitalized. Without him the venture didn't succeed. Then his second wife left him for a younger man. They went to California, taking my two half brothers with them. After a few years of driving a taxi, my father's entrepreneurial spirit resurfaced. He bought a Mercedes-Benz service station franchise and two more taxis. He was just starting to become successful again, and then he died. We buried him in Montreal. Mom dressed him in the new suit he'd bought to wear if she agreed to remarry him.

It was very sad.

After about a year of modeling in Toronto, I decided it was time to try to get into television. Armed with my success as a ballroom dance teacher at the Arthur Murray studios in Ottawa, I had the idea that I could also teach ballroom dancing on television. I watched daytime TV talk shows, and I decided that teaching people to dance would be a natural broadcast segment.

I managed to get an appointment with Dodi Robb, a pioneer of Canadian television and one of TV's few female executives. At that time, she was producer of CFTO's morning show. She liked my idea for a dance segment and gave me a chance.

I appeared once a week, around nine thirty in the morning, and taught the cameras to dance the foxtrot, the cha-cha, and the waltz. I had graphics created showing the various steps, and I asked the audience to write in to receive them by mail. Within six months we were getting close to a thousand letters a week.

Six months later, when Dodi became executive producer of CBC network's afternoon show *Take 30*, she took my segment and me with her. The show was first hosted by Anna Cameron and Paul Soles, and later by Soles and Adrienne Clarkson—all well-known Canadian television personalities. My segment became very successful. I soon had the Friday show's cohost spot, teaching Paul Soles—and Canada—how to dance.

Both my mom and Brigitte's mom had now moved to Toronto. We all lived together for a little while, in a one-bedroom suite, then we got separate apartments in the same building: Brigitte with her mom and I with mine.

Mom and I got Koko, a black-and-white French minia-ture poodle. I now had a steady income from CBC, but it was not enough to live on, so Mom and I decided to go into business together. We started a ballet school, renting a space above a bank at the corner of Mt. Pleasant and Eglinton Avenue.

After buying a used piano, we held auditions for an accompanist. Because we couldn't afford professionals, we auditioned students from the conservatory. They were not very good. After listening to a few, Mom said that she could do better—and she did.

We became perfect partners. She did the books and played piano, and I was the dance teacher. We used my TV work for publicity.

It was hair-raising waiting for our first customer. But gradually the kids came, and the Agota Gabor School of Dancing was born. Within a year, we had more than one hundred students. We were making a living, and we were confident we would grow.

Mom also got a part-time job at the Eglinton Theatre. She sold popcorn at first, but after her English improved she became assistant manager. The film playing at the time was Mike Todd's *Around the World in 80 Days*.

Then the disco craze hit Toronto.

A dancer from New York came to teach disco dancing in the supper club of the Inn on the Park, the second hotel in the now-famous Four Seasons Hotel chain. I read about her success and went to see her show three times, learned all I needed, and then got a job teaching disco at the very fashionable Anndore House on Charles Street in Midtown. It was great fun teaching the frog, the swim, the chicken, and all the other crazy moves. I was also making very good money, and I made even more doing one-off club dates teaching disco and leading the dancing at private parties.

One job was a party at Eaton Hall, in King City. The Eatons are one of Canada's oldest and richest families— Canadian royalty, essentially—and Eaton Hall, now a museum, is Toronto's Buckingham Palace. I remember charging them five hundred dollars for the evening. When I arrived, Lady Eaton, the family matriarch, sent her butler to bring me to meet her. She was very old but very kind, and said she simply wanted to meet the girl with the guts to charge her five hundred dollars to teach a dance.

I also auditioned for and got a wonderful contract from CBC. They gave me a spot in an elaborate live variety show called *The CBC Concert Party*, created to entertain the UN troops overseas—the Canadian version of Bob Hope's USO tours. Our first trip was to the Gaza Strip in the Middle East.

We flew out from the Trenton air base in a huge Hercules transport plane and sat with our backs to the side of the plane. We all wore earplugs (which looked like today's fancy headphones) because the noise was deafening.

We first stopped in Pisa, Italy, saw the Leaning Tower, and were surprised to meet many tall Italians. In Toronto most of the Italian immigrants came from southern Italy, where men and women tend to be shorter. It felt great being back in Europe, and even though I couldn't speak Italian, everything seemed familiar, so much like back home. Landing anywhere in Europe still feels familiar to me.

Our next stop was Lebanon. We toured Lebanon, going to see the Baalbek ruins and Beirut, a beautiful city (this was before it was torn apart by civil war). We went to the lavish casino and saw elaborately dressed sheikhs playing baccarat, winning and losing thousands of dollars.

We were also taken to the Gaza refugee camp. It was terribly dirty, crowded with people who had nothing. I saw poverty like I had never seen before. In the dust and heat, clusters of hungry kids stood begging. They hung on to our bus as it drove past, and when we got out they hung on to us too.

They were playing a cruel game with a puppy, swinging him around so he'd hit the wall. We tried to stop them, and then they put the puppy in front of our bus so we couldn't leave. One of the musicians grabbed the pup and we took him with us. He was adopted by the Canadian headquarters in Rafah Camp and lived there for years.

We visited a children's hospital in Gaza. I still have a picture of me and our bandleader, Lucio Agostini, holding a three-month-old baby. I look at the photo from time to time and wonder what happened to that baby. He would be about fifty years old today.

I traveled with the Concert Party off and on for the next five years. We made several more trips to the Middle East, as well as to Germany, France, and all over Canada. I worked hard to keep my legs strong, always remembering Dr. Pető, who told me that I should never stop working on my muscles and that my fight against the poliovirus would never end.

My last performance with the Concert Party was in 1968 in Alert, located on Ellesmere Island, Nunavut, near the North Pole. It's the northernmost inhabited place on earth.

We first landed at the American base in Greenland. We did a show there to repay their hospitality; the next morning we were to fly north. The next day the weather turned bad, and our American hosts as well as the Canadian flight crew wanted us performers to decide whether to move on to Alert or cancel the flight. We voted to go. The flight was hair-raising. "Bumpy" wouldn't describe it. We all prayed in our own way. Moe Koffman, the great sax player of "Swinging Shepherd Blues" fame, put on his yarmulke and knelt; Peter Appleyard, the legendary composer and percussionist, knelt next to him. It was very scary.

We made it.

Alert was very cold, but so dry that you didn't feel it. The soldiers came with us for short walks in the twenty-four-hour darkness, but they made us go inside after a few minutes because you could get frostbite without even realizing it. We were glad we took the risk to get there and do the performance. The guys needed a break, and they enjoyed our Christmas program. The show's star and MC was Tommy Hunter, a well-loved Canadian country music singer of the time. Then there was me and one other dancer, a female singer, and a wonderful big band featuring Peter Appleyard on drums and Moe Koffman on sax. The venue was a lot smaller than the US camp in Greenland, but the close to one hundred soldiers made for a great audience.

When not traveling with the Concert Party, I was still doing some shows on weekends and performed regularly at the resort areas of Mont-Tremblant, near Montreal. On one of my trips, while walking on St. Catherine Street, I bumped into Ferenc, the boy I had met and fallen in love with years before in the refugee camp in Austria. He said that after arriving in Halifax in 1957, he came to Montreal and looked for me. He couldn't find me, and his family arranged for him to go to the University of Wyoming. He had graduated and was now back in Montreal, working at a club as maître d'hôtel. For me it was like a "thunderbolt," as love at first sight is described in the movie *The Godfather*. This was love at second sight, but as I looked at Ferenc on St. Catherine Street, I wanted him to be mine forever.

We started our romance long distance. I took the train to Montreal almost every week, and Ferenc started looking for a job in Toronto. Six months later he got one, and he moved to Toronto.

Count Ferenc Nádasy was from one of Hungary's oldest aristocratic families. His family history went back one thousand years. In Canada he didn't use his title, but I was still impressed by his ancestry. Ferenc was great looking, with dark hair and hazel eyes, slim and effortlessly, casually elegant. He had a deep voice and spoke beautiful English. Interestingly, we almost never spoke Hungarian to each other and never called each other by name. We just called each other "darling." He was smart and was also a dreamer. He wanted to be a writer and photographer. I'd become more of a realist by that time, but I was in love and not realistic when it came to being with him.

In Toronto, Ferenc got a job as assistant catering manager at the Inn on the Park hotel. And, much to her dislike, Mom and Ferenc and I rented a small three-bedroom house on Edith Drive and moved in together. The house had a finished basement, which Ferenc made into his art studio. It worked well for a few months, because we were all working and our different schedules gave us each some space. But soon Mom and Ferenc started fighting and the arrangement had to change.

We decided to get married. Maybe I decided that more than he did, but he went along and I knew he loved me. We went to Toronto's beautiful Old City Hall to get married. It was a very small wedding, and we had a small outdoor reception at a hotel on the lakeshore. Our closest friends were there: Brigitte and her mom; my brother, Frank, and his then-new wife, Lou, and her three-year-old girl, Theresa; our friend Zeev; Ferenc's old friend Laci; and of course my mom. We couldn't afford to go away for a honeymoon; instead, we looked for an apartment for us and renovated the space behind our dance studio into a small apartment for Mom. It worked.

Ferenc and I were very happy. We were both good-looking and we knew it. We made enough money to live and have fun. It was the early sixties, and our one-bedroom apartment was near Yorkville, Toronto's home for hippies and very good music. We hung out with Hungarian friends, with dancers, models, and some waiters from the club where Ferenc worked. We had a hard-working, young, bohemian lifestyle. I never cooked, and we spent any free nights we had at the now-iconic Riverboat Café, seeing performers like Gordon Lightfoot and Joni Mitchell.

Mom didn't like Ferenc and thought him entitled because of his aristocratic background. She also said he was anti-Semitic, which I didn't want to believe. My relationship with Mom became strained because of my marriage. Since she and Koko lived in the apartment behind our dance studio, we saw each other most days, but I knew she was not pleased with me and Ferenc and she wanted a different life for me.

I was hoping they would eventually get along, but in my heart, I too was worried about the long-term prospects for my marriage. I was ambitious and impatient to establish a life for us. I wanted to make money and have a career, while Ferenc wanted to go to Spain to write a book. I feared that Ferenc and I had different life goals: I wanted to make a life in Canada; Ferenc wanted to wait out the Soviet occupation so he could go back to Hungary. But all this was an undercurrent, because we loved each other and our life together.

In 1965, Hungary gave amnesty to the two hundred thousand Hungarians who fled after the 1956 revolution. Mom decided to go home to see her sisters, and I was determined to go with her, but we didn't have enough money for two return airfares.

I had an idea, which I pitched to my boss and mentor, Dodi Robb.

I told her that I now had a viewership and a following on *Take 30* because of my Friday dance lessons. Wouldn't they like to see a documentary, hosted by me, on how the lives of women and children in Communist Hungary compared to those of their Canadian counterparts?

Dodi liked the idea and gave me a contract. *Take 30* would pay airfare for a film crew and me and gave us a budget of two thousand dollars.

I asked two other Hungarian friends, a cameraman and a film director, if they would be interested in going back home for free, in exchange for shooting two mini-documentaries. They were happy to do it. I was more than excited getting ready for my big trip—going home to

Budapest, and as the producer-interviewer of my first-ever television documentary.

This was a very big step for me, and a big gamble Dodi was taking on me. At that time, I had experience in front of the camera and in TV chitchat about dancing on *Take 30*. But I knew nothing about television production. I was trusting my instincts and my smarts in hiring two very talented and professional people to guide me.

One Sunday afternoon, when we were still making our preparations for the trip, Ferenc showed me an article in the *Toronto Telegram* about a CBC show called *News Magazine*. It was an interview with the producer Don Cameron, about a documentary he'd recently shot about life in the Soviet Union.

"You should call him," Ferenc said. "Since you are going to Hungary anyway, maybe he would like to have you do something for *News Magazine* too?"

I called Don Cameron the next day. He said that since he'd just gotten back from the Soviet Union, I should really talk to Bill Cunningham, who would be producing the next show. He said he would have Mr. Cunningham call me.

Mr. Cunningham called the next day. He said his boss told him to call me and wanted to know what I wanted. I told him I was doing two film segments for *Take 30* in Hungary and was wondering if *News Magazine* would be interested in having me shoot something for them while we were over there. He asked me what kind of cameras we were using.

I figured out that he was testing me, wanting to know if I knew anything about filming. I didn't, but I quickly told him I would have my cameraman discuss the details with him; but more important, what type of segment would he like us to shoot? He said he would decide on the content and I'd better come to his office for an interview.

The *News Magazine* offices were on Jarvis Street, next door to TV Studio 6, where I taped my *Take 30* show every week. The office was on the fifth floor, next to the TV newsroom. I was shown to Mr. Cunningham's office. As I waited at the door, I saw a guy with movie-star good looks on the phone inside, with his feet on his desk. He waved me to a chair. Soon he hung up and, without taking his feet off the desk, told me that it was his mother who had called him and that he really didn't want to talk to her because he had a terrible hangover.

I told him I was having trouble seeing his face. He asked me why, and I told him his feet were in the way.

It wasn't a good start. The strangest thing about the meeting wasn't his brusque style or my impertinence, it was that all I kept thinking was what it would be like being married to him. I brushed that thought away and instead told him why he should hire me to host a show on Hungary for *News Magazine.*

I told him that I had been a student at the Academy of Drama and Film and before that had studied ballet at the opera house, and that my friends who had stayed in Hungary were now actresses, dancers, and filmmakers. I explained how interesting it would be to compare their lives in Hungary to mine in Canada. He liked the idea and took me to Craigleigh Gardens, in Rosedale, to do a mock interview filmed by his cameraman. After we were done, he dropped me off at a subway station, saying he had to run but would let me know how the camera liked me and how the interview came across.

He called two days later and said all went well and looked good. He agreed to do the segment. "Talk contract with accounting," he said. "I'm leaving for Paris in two days."

Accounting gave me the contract. I was to do the research, set up and do all the interviews, and host the program. Mr. Cunningham was to produce and direct. I was going to be paid $1,200, plus expenses.

It was a very busy time for me: getting ready for my trip, taping *Take 30* every week, and planning a recital for the students at the ballet school. We were staging *The Fairy Doll*, the one-act ballet by Bayer, which tells the story of the toys and dolls in a toy store on Christmas Eve as the fairy doll brings them alive to dance. Because I used to dance various parts as a kid in Budapest, I knew the choreography. We rented a big theater at the University of Toronto; my friend Zeev, who once worked at the Folies Bergère in Paris, helped with the lighting; and we all worked hard on our dance studio's first big show.

The whole *News Magazine* project *and* Mr. Cunningham seemed surreal. Bill and I had one more meeting, a lunch, the day before my recital and his departure for Europe. We met at the Four Seasons Hotel across the street from the CBC studios on Jarvis Street.

It was an interesting lunch. I remember I wore a green silk suit and had my hair done. I was dressed to impress, and I was nervous. To me he was a big shot, and I thought he had acted like one the last time we met.

This time our meeting was different. He was polite. No feet on the table, no hangover. He wore a light beige suit and looked very sophisticated. I asked what I should prepare for the shoot, and he told me to think of questions to ask of politicians and my friends. I asked if I needed to bring special clothes, and he asked me if I had a Burberry trench coat. I said I didn't, and he told me to buy one and put it down as an expense. I was surprised and asked if he was serious. He was. He said, "All foreign correspondents wear trench coats." He then leaned over, looked deep into my eyes, and said, "You will make a beautiful correspondent." I laughed and said thank you. But I felt that look all the way through my body down to my heels. I knew in that instant that there was going to be more than work in this relationship.

We said goodbye and agreed to meet at the Hotel Gellért, in Budapest, three weeks later.

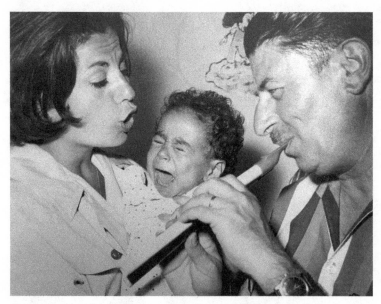

Concert Party conductor Lucio Agostini and me when visiting a hospital in Gaza

Singer Shirley Harmer and me with the UN troops in the desert

Teaching Take 30 *host Paul Soles to dance on television*

Mom at work at Toronto's Eglinton Theatre

CHAPTER 6

LA BOLSHE VITA

I was very excited about my first trip back to Europe. I made plans to stop in Paris for four days on my way to Budapest. Going to Paris was my childhood dream, and I'd always wanted to do it on my own. This was my chance.

My happiness about the trip was almost destroyed by a big fight I had with Ferenc a few nights before I was to leave. He usually finished his job at Julie's Mansion around 1:00 a.m. and was home by 2:00. But he came home at 4:00, obviously not sober, and I accused him of being with a girl who also worked at the bar. We didn't speak for a couple of days, and then it was time for me to leave. We only made up the morning of my departure. He took me to the airport and I almost missed my plane. He kissed me goodbye, and all of a sudden I didn't want to leave; I had a panicked feeling that this was the last time I would ever kiss him like that. I felt that part of my life ending, right at that very moment. The Air Canada attendant finally said I had to go or I would miss my flight. Ferenc and I looked at each other a final time, and I ran to the plane.

"The sky is always blue above the clouds" is a Hungarian saying. As I looked out the window of the plane before it started its descent into Paris, the saying had never felt truer. The sun was shining above the clouds as French music played over the airplane's sound system. Then came the announcement that we were landing at Charles de Gaulle Airport. I was so happy I cried.

I booked a room at the Hôtel de Paris Opéra, across the street from the opera house. During the next days, I walked all over the city. I saw all the sights I had dreamed of seeing. I even took a dance class at a studio in Montmartre. I went to the Louvre and to the Musée d'Orsay, I toured the opera, went to Versailles and to Notre-Dame cathedral. I walked the Champs-Élysées and window-shopped. I went to the top of the Eiffel Tower and looked over the rooftops of Paris, which seemed to be just like I'd expected from the many pictures I'd looked at as a kid. I had red wine in many small bars and cafés, and fresh pastries and croissants. It was just as I knew it would be. The four days flew by. Then I took the two-hour flight home to Budapest.

Budapest is one of the most beautiful cities in the world. I thought so when it was the only big city I knew, and I still feel the same way after having seen many others over the years.

Budapest was born in 1872, when the areas of Pest, Buda, and Old Buda were amalgamated. It had a population of 150,000 then, and now it is more than three million. It's no wonder that Budapest is one of the most photogenic cities in the world: it's peppered with nineteenth-century architectural wonders, including the majestic Hungarian Parliament Building, the thirteenth-century Matyas Church, the Fisherman's Bastion, and the Buda Castle. The city is known as the Queen of the Danube, and the river is its lifeblood. Eight beautiful bridges connect Buda and Pest, among them the historic Széchenyi Chain Bridge, built in 1849. The withdrawing Germans destroyed all the bridges in 1945, but they all have been rebuilt. The Chain Bridge reopened a hundred years after its original opening, on January 20, 1949.

Andrássy Avenue is one of the city's main thoroughfares, a spacious, lovely road lined with trees and bordered with magnificent villas and historic buildings. St. Stephen's Basilica is at one end, Heroes' Square at the other, and the Budapest Opera House in between. As I used to live near there, these landmarks were something of a backyard to me. I used to play hopscotch on Heroes' Square and spent most of my childhood days at the opera house.

Flying into the city almost ten years after leaving it as a teenager—fearing I would never be allowed to come back—was an emotional experience. Budapest still looked like home, but it seemed so much smaller than I remembered from when I left.

The airport was a hug-and-kiss marathon. Everybody was kissing someone. I wondered if they were just kissing people randomly until they found their own family! All my aunts, my uncle Geza, and my cousin Zoli were there to meet me; we did a lot of kissing of our own.

I spent a fantastic two weeks in Budapest. I stayed with my aunt Klara and uncle Geza, whom I had stayed in touch with over the years, and I met with many other family members and friends. It was a wonderful feeling to be with them and to be at home. I went back to the apartment building I grew up in and was standing in the courtyard, looking up at the fourth floor, when the janitor recognized me. He called the family living in our old apartment and told them I was in town, and they let me go in to see our old home. Apart from some new furniture, it looked just as I remembered. I went out to the small balcony from where my brother, Frank, and I used to sprinkle water on passersby. The view was the same. It was so nice of that family to allow me in: it gave me a special moment, a quick window back into my childhood.

I went back to the opera house and watched my friends rehearse. Many of them were now soloists with the Hungarian State Opera Company. It was wonderful to be back, and to be back while working for a Canadian television network was even better. My friends were duly impressed. They were curious about my life. I think a couple of them felt jealous and kind of sad, saying they missed their chance when they decided not to leave Hungary in '56. I too felt some mixed emotions. I was proud and happy with my life, but at the same time, seeing them dance the roles I always wanted to dance but would never be able to made me envious.

We started work setting up shots for the two segments for *Take 30*. I had to reach out to contacts, do pre-interviews, find interviewees who could speak English, and set up shoots. All this had to be done in Hungarian, which I had never dreamt would be a problem.

Why would it be? I'd been away for only ten years, and I still used Hungarian when speaking with Mom and some friends. But for the first few days it certainly was difficult. I spoke fluently, but like a teenager instead of the adult I was. I also had difficulty reading the papers and talking about

politics; for some of the words, I needed to use a dictionary
to understand.

As the days went by it got easier, but I had to think it
through and choose my words, especially when speaking on
the telephone. It reminded me of my first years in Canada,
when I was learning English: speaking on the telephone,
with no facial expressions and gestures to help, was difficult
then too.

Miki, my cameraman; Jani, the director; and I started
filming for the *Take 30* segments and shot generic visuals
of the city. We also researched locations and interviewees
for the upcoming shoot for *News Magazine*, to be directed
by Bill Cunningham. The *News Magazine* show would focus
on the difference in the lives of young people in Hungary
and Canada, as well as the broader economic, cultural, and
political state of Hungary ten years after the revolution. The
regime in the sixties was called Goulash Communism; it was
a little less rigid than the regimes that ruled East Germany
and the other Soviet satellites. Many people thought that
this was because the revolution of '56 was so bloody. The
government didn't want to provoke bloodshed like that
again.

A Hungarian "fixer" named George was attached to our
crew by the government. He was a small, dark-haired man
who said he was a researcher there to help us, but we knew
that he would be reporting to the government everything we
did or said. He was there to make sure we did exactly what
we promised, and didn't do or say anything negative about
the system, which was a bit more lenient than when I'd left
the country, but was a dictatorship with few freedoms just
the same. George was a funny person and certainly knew
ways to get around the archaic bureaucracy. He reminded

me of the popular saying in Canada, "Watch the Hungarian who is behind you in a revolving door; he will somehow come out ahead."

I was to meet Mr. Cunningham at the Hotel Gellért, one of the classic establishments known as the Ladies of the Danube. The Gellért opened in 1918, after the First World War, as the Hungarian empire descended into chaos. It was famous for its art nouveau decor and also for its thermal baths. As a child I spent many Sundays enjoying its indoor and outdoor pools.

I went to the hotel bar to wait for Mr. Cunningham, enjoying my many memories.

He showed up half an hour late, perfectly dressed and handsome as ever, with a trench coat on his arm. He profusely apologized, explaining he had a bad hangover and had overslept after taking a nap. He also mentioned his ulcers were acting up due to a very late night in Paris the day before.

I was disappointed. This job was important to me; it was a chance to take a big step forward in my career and my future. He, on the other hand, didn't seem to be taking the project very seriously. I told him there was a great Hungarian hangover cure, and I took him to a restaurant famous for its spicy fish soup. *That should fix his ulcers,* I thought.

Bill gave me a kind of lopsided smile and said, "I am in your hands. Show me your city."

After dinner at the aptly named Százéves (Hundred-Year-Old) Restaurant, we went to the Moulin Rouge nightclub in the theater district and watched a production of *Happy Days Are Here Again,* which was the political message of the time.

We drove around Budapest: around Old Buda; into the hills to the castle where Franz Joseph, emperor of Austria and king of Hungary, once lived; on to Aquincum, the former ancient city where the Roman ruins still stand; and then back to Pest, to the famous and most beautiful parliament in all of Europe. We ended up in Heroes' Square, where the seven chieftains of the Magyar tribes are overseen by the enormous Archangel Gabriel column.

I showed Bill where I used to live on the Kodály körönd, named after the famous composer Zoltán Kodály. We then took the Little Subway, Europe's oldest, with only two cars. I used to take it to school every day.

We strolled around the opera house, where I told him about growing up there, and then we walked across the Freedom Bridge toward his hotel. It was a very nice evening. A good start for our work together, I thought. He then surprised me by kissing me good night. Going home to my aunt's house, I was happy but worried. Was this going to be an affair—and was I ready to have one? I didn't know. I was infatuated with Bill, but I didn't want to get too deeply involved.

We made a date to meet for lunch on the terrace of the Hotel Gellért the next day. The crew and our fixer, George, would join us.

We started shooting the following day. I was impressed by Bill's instinctive understanding of my country's issues and what was important to film, seemingly without having done any research. He had a great eye for visuals, he knew what he wanted in the film, and he was professional with the crew. I learned a lot very quickly while working with him.

Later I introduced him to my family: my mom, who was also there visiting; my aunts and my uncle; and my cousins. While they really couldn't communicate in depth, they thought he was great. He was Canadian, and to them, being "from the West" was impressive. He was good-looking and he was a journalist and in television. My aunt Klara's way of communicating with Bill was to give him cakes and espresso whenever he came to pick me up from her house, where both my mom and I were staying.

My uncle Geza was a journalist and a member of Parliament. He was also a Communist long before it was fashionable to be one. As a Communist and a Jew, he was taken into forced labor during World War II, but Soviet Army soldiers went across the front line to retrieve him and take him to the Soviet side. He came back to Budapest after the war as a lieutenant in the Soviet Army.

Geza had arranged for us to interview the prime minister; he also helped us set up shoots in the parliament building and the Csepel steel factory, the largest and newest factory in Hungary. At the factory, my uncle told us a popular joke of the time:

"Why don't they have strikes in Hungary?" he asked. "Because if they did, when they stopped working, nobody would notice."

We filmed my aunt Klara shopping at the Lehel Market, an outdoor market where I interviewed her and other shoppers about prices and the availability of different foods. We also filmed my young cousin, Zoli, at an international youth meet at a camp in the Buda Hills. He told me how the Socialist pioneer movement had changed since I was a member in the fifties.

We filmed a short sequence in the rehearsal hall of the opera, with three of my former classmates and me doing a short warm-up at the ballet barre, which I loved.

We also shot various street scenes showing the bullet holes on many of the buildings, remnants of both the Second

World War and the '56 revolution. The revolution was then called the counterrevolution, and the government line was that it was all planned by antigovernment forces that took advantage of the peaceful student demonstrations to start an armed revolt. Any suggestion that life was perhaps a little better because of the revolution was denied.

The technique we used to show the many parts of Budapest was to film me crisscrossing the city by streetcar. Bill wanted to show me jumping on and off the streetcars, as most Hungarians do, and this is where my old problems caused by polio showed up. I could only jump off a streetcar using my left leg—the other way I would more than likely fall—so I asked Bill to shoot the scene in only one direction.

He didn't understand, since I hadn't told him I had suffered from polio. He just knew me as a dancer, so it was hard for him to understand why jumping off a streetcar would be a problem. I realize now that my illness should not have embarrassed me, but I was so eager to do everything perfectly that I tried to cover up the truth. I fibbed and told him I had a sore knee that day, and we made do.

We also shot a dinner-party scene at the renowned Citadel restaurant, which sits on top of Gellért Hill and boasts possibly the best panoramic view of the city.

I invited some of my friends, beginning with Koko—my fellow ballet rat, best friend, and former competitor, who was now a soloist at the opera house—and her husband, who was a conductor at the symphony. I also asked Margit, from my class at the academy, who was now an actress; her partner, a doctor; and my friend Eric, a young architect, and his girlfriend.

The dinner party gave me the platform to interview each of them. We talked about where they lived, their apartments, and asked if they had a television, if they traveled, and whether they were able to save money. These simple questions got at the important distinction between their lives and mine and those of others like me of the same age in Canada.

The prime minister's office had granted us an interview only if Bill conducted it instead of me. They said it would be like Burgess and Maclean (known as the Cambridge Spies) interviewing former British Foreign Minister Anthony Eden. We just laughed it off, and they invited me to listen to the interview and meet the prime minister.

The crew, my friends, and my family all suspected that Bill and I had started dating, and they knew that we were both married, but they didn't seem to see anything wrong with it.

My girlfriends thought Bill was great; they just laughed and said, "Enjoy your *chassé*," which is a step in ballet and is also what Hungarians often call an affair. After all, they said, when should you have fun, if not now? We were all in our mid-twenties. I was twenty-six.

My uncle Geza was the only one in my family who asked me what was going on between Bill and me and warned me of the consequences. He suggested that all this glitter of filming with a television crew and being courted by a sophisticated man may have turned my head. He said that if I still loved my husband, I should be careful not to lose him. I knew somewhere deep inside that he was right, but by then I was too involved and an affair sounded wonderful.

To close out the program, Bill had rented a watering truck to make the cobblestoned streets of the old city look wet with rain, and for the final scene he had me slowly walk through them in a trench coat.

I will never forget my voice-over narration: "I am a tourist in my country—a tourist who speaks the language, but a tourist after all."

Finally, Bill had me stand at the bow of the Danube hydrofoil leaving for Vienna, with the wind blowing through my hair.

Who would not have fallen in love with him? I sure did.

We named the show *La Bolshe Vita*.

After we finished the shoot, Bill moved on to Prague to do another documentary, and I went with him. We stayed for a week. I hung out with the film crew and met some interesting artists. We also saw the famous glass-blowing factory, and Bill and I spent some wonderful times together. I enjoyed myself, and I loved the adventure. Bill said he was in love and wanted me to leave my husband. I wasn't sure. I didn't say it to him, but in my head, I had figured on our involvement staying as an affair, nothing more.

After Prague we went to London for a day, and then we said goodbye.

Before we parted, Bill said he was going to leave both his wife *and* his girlfriend, and he said I should leave Ferenc right away and then we should marry. It sounded dashing and daring.

But more than anything, it sounded scary.

*Dinner with friends at
the Citadel in Budapest*

Me and Bill in Budapest

Bill Cunningham

CHAPTER 7

BACK TO SCHOOL

My trip to Hungary led me to several crossroads.

I had to choose between staying married and getting a divorce. I had to choose whether to stay with the world of dance, grow my school, and try to break into choreography, or pivot to television production and journalism.

I loved Ferenc, and I wasn't going to tell him about my affair. I wanted to give our marriage another try, but sadly the wife of my cameraman for the Hungary shoot told him that I went to Prague with Bill. When I got back to Toronto and home, Ferenc asked to see my passport. There it was: the stamp of entry to Czechoslovakia.

After the first shock, Ferenc told me he was hurt but wanted to give it another try to work things out, but I felt guilty and afraid. I somehow knew that our marriage couldn't survive my affair and I didn't want to lose them both. After a few hard days of painful discussions, Ferenc and I separated. We needed time, and I wanted to move out and live alone.

I was fascinated by and admired Bill Cunningham, but I really didn't know him well. It is true that one can love two men at the same time—that seemed to be the case for me, anyway. For a long and very stressful time, I couldn't decide what to do. My mom really liked Bill and was hoping I would end up with him; she said she believed I had a future with him, and that brought on fights between us. Bill was also pressuring me, since he'd left his wife and he said he'd also left his girlfriend. I felt under pressure to make life choices I wasn't ready to make. All the stress made me start neglecting my work at the dance studio. I was often late for my classes, and Mom would have to play the warm-up music and direct the kids until I arrived. She was furious. What's more, my eating disorder came back and I was emotionally drained. I was still working with Bill editing *La Bolshe Vita*, and on the days I didn't see him, I was dating Ferenc, with whom I was still in love in a painful way. It was exhausting and too much for me to handle.

It seemed like everyone was pulling me in a different direction. The person I relied on as my rock was my friend Zeev. A hopeless romantic when it came to his own life, he was practical when it came to mine. Ferenc and I met Zeev Fried at the Riverboat Café in Yorkville, where he was one of the dishwashers. When he heard us speak Hungarian, he came over to meet us. Zeev was a Hungarian Jew who escaped from Auschwitz when he was thirteen. He lost his whole family in the camps, and when he made his way back to Hungary, he found that everyone he knew in Miskolc, his hometown, had also been murdered by the Nazis. Zeev made his way to Israel, joined the army, and fought in the 1948 Arab-Israeli War. He then went to Paris and managed to get a job from a fellow Hungarian who was the artistic director of the famous Paris nightclub the Folies Bergère. Zeev told us he loved that job, but his ladylove moved to Montreal and he followed her there. The affair didn't work out, and he came to Toronto to start a new life. He decided to become a chef. Undaunted by his lack of experience, he got a job as a dishwasher at the Riverboat. Sure enough, he worked hard and learned quickly, and soon he rose to become assistant chef. A year later he became chef at another Yorkville restaurant. Zeev was smart, funny, and outrageous. With a crooked smile, he would tell everyone that his great-great-great-great-grandfather was the food taster for Louis XIV, and that gourmet food was in his genes.

When Ferenc and I split up, Zeev became my best friend and confidant.

He reminded me that I couldn't afford to be a lovesick romantic; I had to make money. He constantly asked me if I'd forgotten that I was an immigrant and had to make a living. "Who do you think you are, Anna Karenina?" he would say. It was with his help that I started looking for job opportunities again. I got in touch with everyone I knew at CBC, and with the two film segments for *Take 30* and the very successful documentary I made with Bill for *News Magazine*, I had some experience and a reasonable résumé. I got lucky, and in a short time and with Bill's help, I landed a temporary job as a script assistant in the news department. I was told that if I did well, I would be considered for a permanent position.

I took to the job like a fish to water. Live television is exciting. In the newsroom you have a first-row seat to what's happening in the world.

I worked at the TV newsroom on the fifth floor of the old CBC building on Jarvis Street. The staff of a TV newsroom is split between those who gather and write the news, and those who put it on air. The writers, reporters, and editors decide the content of the newscast; the production team makes it happen and presents it live on air.

The production team is further split into two groups. The technical producer and his crew are one group. The other group comprises the news director, his floor director, and the script assistant, who are in charge of how content is presented.

Script assistants—or "scripts," as we were called—had many responsibilities. Some were exciting and some were boring.

My shift would begin when the assignment editor gave me the news lineup. From there I'd figure out the list of graphics, music, and sound effects needed for the evening news.

When the script was ready, about a half hour before air-time, we could all hear the loud voice of the show writer shouting, "Split, please!" Back then the script for the news program was typewritten on five sheets of green paper with four carbon copies attached. The copyboy split the script and collated it into five complete copies: one for the anchor, one for the news writer, one for the director, one for the script assistant, and one for the studio director.

The script consisted partly of contributions from reporters, and partly of other pieces from continuity writers. The director added notes indicating which parts were to be read by the news anchor on camera or as voice-overs, and marked visuals as slides, film, or videotape. Then the lengths and "in and out" cues of the different film and tape segments were marked. Next the script was given to me, the script assistant. I would time all the segments. A two-column script takes around thirty seconds to read. I needed to time all the pages, add the total time to the combined lengths of all the film and video segments, include any live-interview times, and make sure the script fit the length of the show. If it was light or heavy, I gave it to the writer to be adjusted.

Just before airtime, I had to make sure all graphics were correct and ready and give the music and sound effects to Telecine for the film items or VTR for the videotapes. Silence was not allowed during the newscast. We had music for floods, earthquakes, happy scenes, sad stories, and neutral information.

During the broadcast I sat in the control room, to the left of the director. The director called the shots, and the script assistant informed everyone what was to come: graphic, video, film, or an interview. The script assistant also kept everyone aware of both segment time and overall time, and communicated with the studio director on the floor, who passed necessary information on to the show's anchor.

Timing the show and adjusting it for length, often on the fly, was difficult and important. Being good and quick with numbers was a must for a script assistant, and I was good at it. Interestingly, most people who speak more than one language automatically revert to their mother tongue when they're under pressure. So when I switched to counting in Hungarian, the control room fell silent. The director would whisper, "Quiet, please—she switched to Hungarian. We may be in trouble."

I loved my job. There is nothing quite like the adrenaline rush of working on a live broadcast. Looking back on all the different jobs I've had in my life, being a "script" was one of the best. Working in the newsroom, I slowly realized that this was the world I wanted to be a part of going forward. Perhaps this was the plan B of my life, after polio destroyed my dancing dreams.

Meanwhile Bill and I were getting closer, and I knew that, both professionally and personally, my life was changing.

One evening at dinner, Bill asked if I was serious about becoming a journalist. I said yes. He said that if I was, I should go back to school. He said I was good and quick in production, but if I really wanted to get ahead, I should also learn to write for the news, and also learn about politics and economics and what makes news.

Taking advantage of an employee-benefit program CBC had at the time, I enrolled as a mature student in Ryerson University's journalism program. Since the CBC grant paid only for tuition, I still had to make a living. Mom and I had the dance studio, and I had my weekly gig on *Take 30*. Mom also had a part-time job at the Eglinton Theatre, and we had moved in together again, but even so we didn't think there would be enough money for us to live on. We decided to hire a friend and former dancer to help me at the dance studio. I'd keep my job at CBC and also go to school full time.

Ryerson's journalism program was one of the best in Canada. I was ten years older than my classmates, so I didn't really experience the social part of college life and the camaraderie. In truth, even if I'd been seventeen instead of twenty-seven, I wouldn't have had time to socialize. Our classes started at 7:00 or 8:00 a.m. and lasted until 3:00 p.m.

I worked at CBC three weekdays from 3:30 to 11:30 p.m. and on the weekends from 3:00 to 11:20 p.m.

On weekdays I did the 6:00 and 11:20 p.m. local news. On the weekends I did *The National*.

When working on the local news, we were busy from 4:30 to 6:30 p.m., and then we had a dinner break and some downtime until around 9:00 p.m., when things got hectic again. That was my time to study and sleep. Many times I fell asleep in the washroom and my colleagues had to wake me to rush to the studio. It was exhausting but fun. I have always had a lot of energy for what I love, and I tend to thrive amid chaos. With my dramatic and crazy personal life, working and going to school was my solution.

I started at Ryerson in 1966, ten years after I graduated from high school and left Hungary. After my varied, interesting, and at times difficult first ten years in Canada, being back at school was like going back to my youth. I was hungry to learn everything that was offered. I loved political geography and philosophy. In Hungary I had only been exposed to Marxism, which appealed to me as an ideology, but I knew how the principles turned out when applied to everyday life, and so I was realistic and skeptical about it.

I loved working on the student newspaper and found economics interesting. I knew that news writing was important, so it was unfortunate that it was my first class, at 7:00 a.m., and was taught by a former journalist who preferred to tell war stories rather than give us useful information. I enjoyed my young classmates but found them a bit naive for their age. I think we matured earlier in Europe, and certainly historical events in Hungary made that even truer.

English was the subject I needed to work at the most. By this time I was fluent in the spoken language, but since I had learned it only by ear, my grammar and punctuation were atrocious. Our professor was an Englishman in his thirties. I thought him stuffy but knew he was an excellent professor. I tried my best and got a passable mark the first year.

The following year, however, we had a problem. At the time, Bill was a foreign correspondent for CBC, based in Hong Kong. He spent most of his time covering the Vietnam War. He was coming home for an extended Christmas break and invited me to go to Barbados with him for a three-week vacation.

When I told my English professor about my plans, he told me that if I went he would fail me. I told him he couldn't do that if I did the work and passed my exam.

Our reading list for English lit was long. One of the must-reads was *Moby-Dick*, and it was sure to be on the exam. I took all the books with me on my trip with Bill.

We stayed on the West Coast of Barbados, with lovely, gentle beaches and warm, velvet-soft water. It was the first time since Prague that Bill and I had spent any length of time together, and it was one of the best and longest vacations either of us had ever had. Bill was exhausted and on edge, and having nightmares about the war. If he heard a loud voice when he was sleeping, he would jump, thinking it was incoming fire. But after a few days, he relaxed. The Colony Club was luxurious and very British. We spent most of our time on the beach—I, mostly in the water. There was a steel band at lunch and dinner, and we danced to the then-popular Jamaican ska. We went horseback riding and snorkeling and did tours of the island. At night there was entertainment. I didn't have much time to study or read. My thick copy of *Moby-Dick* sat there staring at me from the nightstand, reminding me of my duty. It made me nervous.

Then one night I read the daily pamphlet listing the next day's schedule at the resort, and there I saw "Movie Night: Watch *Moby Dick* under the stars."

I couldn't believe my luck. We watched the movie, and I knew I would not fail my English lit course. Indeed, I passed and made it through the second year of my studies, and soon it was the summer of 1967, Canada's hundredth birthday.

CBC had a department called Outside Broadcasting, which was responsible for the coverage of all state occasions, royal visits, state visits, and royal weddings and funerals. It was the department responsible for all the centennial celebrations.

The dream job that year was to work for Outside Broadcasting. There was a posting for a script assistant in that department, but it required "experience and French and English fluency." I spoke French, but I wasn't fluent. Luckily, because I was from Europe, people just took it for granted that I spoke several languages. I was never tested, and I got the job.

Soon after I started in the department, we attended a large, bilingual kickoff meeting with both the English and French production teams in Montreal. Most of the meeting was conducted in French. My producer and boss didn't speak a word of French, and I was responsible for taking notes on all the proceedings. It was difficult, especially because, as the only young woman in the room, I also had to serve the coffees.

The first show I worked on was *Album of History*, a documentary created from historical photographs depicting highlights of Canada's first hundred years.

An exciting assignment was filming the re-creation of the historical trip of the voyageurs. Our small film crew followed the pioneers on the journey. I had never taken Canadian history in school, and this summer job was better than any university course.

Our next job was to film the centennial train as it weaved through the country to the sounds of various children's choirs singing Bobby Gimby's "Canada." The train was a moving exhibition of the nation's history.

We then spent a week filming highlights of Montreal's Expo 67, shooting visuals of the various pavilions. I distinctly remember that Czechoslovakia's multimedia presentation was amazing, years ahead of its time.

Then we moved to Ottawa for the big day, July 1, and the British royal visit.

A spectacular show was presented to the royals on the outdoor stage in front of the parliament building. We were the unit responsible for broadcasting it live.

Multiculturalism was new to Canada at the time, and the show was a celebration of Canada's diverse cultures: German, Hungarian, Polish, and Finnish Canadians performed. Folk dancers, folk singers, music groups, and gymnasts created a spectacular program, a colorful representation of the varied home countries of new Canadians.

At the end of the show, a representative of each nationality came on stage to be presented to the queen and Prince Philip. The director of our unit was also on stage, and that meant that I was calling the shots.

We had six cameras shooting the event, so our mobile studio had six monitors showing us the various visuals available.

One of the cameras showed Prince Philip chatting with a lovely Finnish gymnast; on another monitor we could see the queen looking at them without a smile. Tempting as it was, we didn't broadcast those images. Instead we cut to a group of schoolchildren in the audience.

The summer of 1967 flew by, and soon it was back to school and work in TV news.

I was working in news in 1968 during the Prague Spring, as the Soviets crushed the Czechs' revolution as they had ours in 1956. It was an emotional time for all of us. I cried in the control room, seeing the streets of Prague full of demonstrators and Soviet soldiers shooting and killing many of them, and remembering when I was ducking bullets with my friends in Budapest.

In the summer of 1968, I got the green light on a show idea I had for CBC Public Affairs. It was similar to my idea for the documentary I did in Hungary, visiting my homeland years after I left it.

My father's family lived in Transylvania, which belonged to Hungary when my father was born but became part of Romania after the Second World War and the Treaty of Versailles. My father's side of the family came from the landed gentry class, which meant they had land and went to war on horseback; our family crest displayed a horse. My paternal great-grandfather was an Orthodox priest, and my grandmother was Armenian.

I'd never met that part of my family, but I'd always wanted to. So I approached the producer of the program *The Public Eye* with a proposal to do a documentary on conditions in Romania under the dictator Ceaușescu, focusing on the Hungarian minority in Transylvania, which I could view through my family's eyes.

I was to work with Charles Wasserman, CBC's European expert based in Austria. He would be the producer, and I would be the host, researcher, and interviewer.

As the researcher, I was to travel to Bucharest a week before the rest of the crew. Before I left on the trip, Mom, who'd spent some time in Romania, gave me her opinion of Romanian men: "Romanian men wear girdles and powder their noses. If a woman allows them to pay for a cup of coffee, they expect her to have sex." *OK, Mom*, I thought.

I arrived in Bucharest late at night, getting to my hotel around 1:00 a.m. There was a lovely terrace restaurant at the hotel, and I was hungry. There was only a Romanian menu, so I ordered something I thought was light.

Then a deep baritone voice asked, "Did you really mean to order sardines and apple pie?" The voice belonged to a very handsome man sitting a couple of tables to my right. I laughed, he joined my table and switched my order from sardines to cheese, and we started talking.

He turned out to be a television director for Romanian state TV, and when I told him I was researching a documentary and would be scouting locations, he offered to give me a quick tour of Bucharest.

Since he'd picked up the tab for our meals, my mother's words about the expectations of Romanian men flashed through my mind.

I decided she was just old-fashioned and accepted his invitation. He had a nice Volkswagen Jetta, and we drove around the city.

Bucharest is a beautiful city, often called the Paris of the East. It even has a small version of the Arc de Triomphe. He showed me the main boulevards, restaurants, the opera house, the theaters, the stadium, and the statues. I truly enjoyed the tour but was getting tired, and I asked him to take me back to the hotel.

He said we were almost there. I looked around and started to get worried. We were in a lovely suburb, not on the main street where my hotel was.

He stopped at a house and said, "I thought you might like a nightcap, to celebrate your first time in Bucharest?"

Now I truly got worried, thinking my mom was right. I said, "No thanks."

He looked at me, laughed, and said, "I had to try, you know. After all, you agreed to come with me for a ride."

He drove me back to the hotel and I was happy to say good night, wondering if he powdered his nose and wore a girdle too!

Transylvania was spectacular. My relatives lived near Braşov in the Carpathian Alps—Dracula country. I had never met them before and didn't know what to expect. I took a train to Braşov and then rented a car to their village. They were very nice to me and impressed that I now lived in Canada and was doing a documentary.

I met my two aunts and two cousins and their two small children. The family was very poor and unhappy, because as Hungarians they were discriminated against in every aspect of their lives.

They lived in an area where 80 percent of the population was Hungarian and yet their kids were not allowed to go to Hungarian school, jobs were hard to get, and as minorities they were paid less than the Romanians doing the same jobs. My family had not had contact with my father for many years, and I had to tell them the news of his death.

I asked my cousin Laci, who was out of work at the time and who spoke Romanian, Hungarian, and English, to be our guide and translator for the show. He agreed, and the next day we headed into the mountains to ask the Carpathian shepherds about Dracula. Some said they didn't know him. Some said he was an American gangster. Some thought he was the chief of the Mafia, and one old man said he knew him well and he could show us his castle.

We took him up on it. The castle really looked like the castle in the Dracula movies, and in fact it became the opening scene of our documentary.

In Bucharest I was joined by the show's producer, Charles Wasserman, the well-known Austro-Canadian journalist who lived in Vienna. His wife, Jackie, and his German cameraman made up our group. Charles had good contacts everywhere in Europe, and working with him was a great learning experience.

We discovered that our paths had crossed before, when he and other foreign journalists met our truck on the way to the Austrian border, back when I was fleeing Budapest during the '56 revolution. When they came by, the Soviet soldiers who were trying to drag us girls into the forest let us go to avoid being seen by the Westerners.

When filming in Bucharest, we stayed in the luxurious Athénée Palace hotel. It had an all-you-can-eat breakfast buffet every morning, with black and red caviar. I never thought you could have too much caviar, but by the third day I learned I was wrong.

We interviewed government officials and journalists and learned that the Romanian regime was much more dictatorial and heavy-handed than Hungary's Goulash Communism of the late sixties. The standard of living was also much lower in Romania than in Hungary in spite of Romania's rich oil fields, which we filmed in Ploiești.

Then we headed to the Black Sea resort of Mamaia, where we stayed in a villa near the magnificent seaside palace of the dictator Nicolae Ceaușescu. Tom Jones's "Delilah" was the big hit at the clubs, and the song was played on a loop, which we found very strange. We also filmed a large group of Gypsies, and I fell in love with a baby girl traveling with them. They urged me to take her with me to Canada. I was tempted but was talked out of it by a much saner Jackie Wasserman.

Back in Toronto I had to face life and my divorce from Ferenc. It was very sad and painful. Ferenc didn't want a divorce and agreed to one only because he finally understood that I was moving on. The process was also far more difficult at that time than it is today. We had to go to court and have a trial, and I had to give my adultery as the reason for Ferenc to divorce me. The judge was a prejudiced old conservative man. To him we were both immigrants, and he probably wished we were still living on the other side of the pond, back where we came from. He asked Ferenc if he was colluding with someone for monetary reasons. Ferenc looked puzzled, and from the back of the courtroom I shouted at the judge, "He doesn't even understand what colluding means, and how dare you say that!" The judge was very mad and turned on me, saying something to the effect of "What do you expect from these people?" He eventually granted the divorce. Ferenc and I went out for a drink and we both cried.

It was ugly and very painful. The pain of that divorce really only left me some twenty years later, when the Berlin wall came down, the Soviet system collapsed, and Ferenc, as predicted, went back to live in Hungary. I had been right. Our lives were moving in two very different directions. He had been marking time for some thirty years, living like an expat, waiting to return home. For me, Canada had become home.

Around the same time, I finished up my studies in journalism. I was sorry to see them come to an end. I was happy to get my diploma and was proud of myself, but I loved Ryerson and was sad to close that chapter of my life. Dave Crombie, Toronto's former mayor and then Ryerson's chancellor, gave me my diploma. I proudly watched years later as Mr. Crombie gave my daughter her diploma, and many years later as he handed an honorary diploma to my husband, Bill.

In June 1969, a week after my graduation, Bill and I got married in a Unitarian church, with Knowlton Nash, Canada's Walter Cronkite, as Bill's best man and Brigitte as my maid of honor. Our reception was given by a friend of Bill's in a mansion in Rosedale, the elegant, gardenlike neighborhood of Toronto. We had around a hundred guests, including the who's who of television journalists of that time, such as Morley Safer and Peter Jennings. It was a fantastic party. Soon after the wedding I had to get ready to leave for Hong Kong.

Bill's posting was going to be anywhere from two to four years, and after that we had no idea where he would be sent. I was getting worried about leaving Mom behind alone in Toronto. I knew it would only be temporary—we had made plans for her to join us in a few months—but it was still very hard. All the same, I was curious and excited about going to the Far East with my handsome foreign-correspondent husband in his ever-present trench coat. Everything seemed a little surreal, as if it were a movie or a dream. It felt a bit like playing a character from my childhood, dancing the part of this grown-up Agota being swept away to the Orient (as Hungarians still referred to the Far East).

CHAPTER 8

HONG KONG

We arrived in Hong Kong in June of 1969.

Landing at the old Kai Tak Airport was like speeding through a narrow alleyway in the sky. The plane seemed so close to the apartment buildings that it felt like we could touch the laundry hanging out to dry.

Kowloon was steaming with humanity; it seemed virtually impossible to move through the throngs of people. We crossed Victoria Harbour on the Star Ferry, passing sampans, steamships, sailboats, and Chinese junks. Approaching Victoria Peak and the modern, bustling island ahead, it seemed like we were arriving on a different planet.

Being in Hong Kong was an overdose for the senses: the crowds; the noise of people, boats, cars, rickshaws, dogs, and mah-jongg; and perhaps most of all the smell, strong with spices, dirt, flowers, fish, animals, and cologne.

The smell is the essence of Hong Kong, so much that when I returned to North America, the air felt dull and empty.

Bill had been living in Hong Kong for a year prior to our marriage. As CBC's correspondent for Southeast Asia, he'd been provided by the network with a lovely large apartment with an office and recording studio attached. The apartment was at 3 Old Peak Road, halfway up the peak, with a large balcony overlooking the busy Hong Kong harbor. It was dazzling, strange, and luxurious.

Bill had a cameraman; a secretary; an *amah*, as they call housekeepers in China; a car and chauffeur; and a dog, a white Pomeranian named Nelson. Bill wanted him to be a sea dog, but he got seasick the minute he was taken on a boat.

The first day we arrived, Bill and I went out to lunch with Ahoy, the chauffeur, and Phillipa, Bill's secretary. Then we went for a drive around town. Hong Kong is one of the most beautiful cities in the world, with everything to offer: ocean, mountains, skyscrapers, and unbelievable shopping, as well as unbelievable poverty. The food we ate was unfamiliar; until I went to Hong Kong, I'd only had North American Chinese food, quite different from the real thing.

It was a great day. I was exhausted and we went home.

In the middle of the night, I was thirsty and walked to the kitchen for a glass of water. I turned on the light, only to be attacked by flying cockroaches. I screamed, of course.

Bill woke up and admonished me: "You shouldn't be in the kitchen. This is Asam's territory. If you want water, you should ask her."

Thanks, I thought. I wasn't allowed in my own kitchen? He later would tell the cockroach story to friends, adding with a laugh that he could always get another wife, but an amah like Asam he could never replace.

Asam ran the show. She was a Vietnamese Chinese woman about fifty years old, who had worked for the family of a French diplomat before joining us. She was a wonderful cook and spoke French and pidgin English. Once I gave up all rights to the running of the house, which was OK with me, we got on fabulously.

Bill and a friend owned a sailboat, a thirty-three-foot Cheoy Lee called *Nordica*. *Nordica* was in the care of Charlie, the boat boy. Charlie grew up in Aberdeen, Hong Kong's city on the water, where thousands live in sampans. The little kids would be lassoed to the boats with loose ropes in order to keep them from falling into the water. Some of the families only tied the boys; I was told girls were not as important. Charlie was autistic but physically highly functional; mentally he was childish, but he was also a sweet and wonderful person. He handled that boat as if it were a toy. I felt safe with him whatever the weather was; he was the best sailor I ever met.

Bill and I spent those first two weeks together in Hong Kong sailing in the South China Sea, swimming off the boat, joining friends on large Chinese junks, shopping in spectacular stores, exploring the small alleys, and sampling street food. It was like a dream.

Sadly, while Hong Kong was home base for Bill, he was reporting from the whole of Southeast Asia and had to spend most of his time in Vietnam, covering the war.

Bill was also planning a big trip culminating in Jakarta, where President Nixon was scheduled for a state visit and talks with Indonesia's President Suharto. The plan was to do stories in the Philippines, Singapore, Malaysia, and then

Indonesia. I was to go along as a researcher and sound assistant.

In 1969 everything was shot on film. We traveled with large 16mm Arriflex cameras, filmstock, sound equipment, lighting, and batteries. The equipment list was endless. There were nine open suitcases, all numbered, lying on the floor of our apartment the night before we left. Nelson, our little dog, was running around the apartment, getting very anxious. He jumped into the suitcases and lifted his leg, preparing to let us know how he felt. We stopped him just in time.

Our first stop was Manila, in the Philippines. It was during the reelection campaign of President Ferdinand Marcos, husband of Imelda with the thousands of shoes. *Time* and *Newsweek* called it the dirtiest, most violent, most corrupt election ever held in the Philippines, where Marcos relied on the three Gs of "guns, goons, and gold" to get votes.

In spite of the colorful markets and the vibrance of the city, violence was everywhere. Our local fixer took us to dinner, and at the entrance we saw a sign: "Please check your firearms." I took a jitney, one of the small, brightly painted city buses, to the local newspaper office to pick up some research materials. The office was a fifteen-minute ride from our hotel. After I talked with the editor, he took me to the door and asked where my driver was. When I told him I came by jitney, he was shocked and told me I was risking my life. He said it was safe to travel only by private cars and taxis, and only with a trusted, known driver.

While in Manila, Bill did an interview with the leader of the opposing liberal party, Sergio Osmeña Jr. Entering his headquarters was like entering a medieval fortress. There were more armed guards at the ready than at the Corleone family compound in *The Godfather*. Later we also shot some visuals of the city and at the memorial of those tortured by the Japanese during the Second World War.

From Manila we flew to Singapore, where we stayed at Raffles, one of the loveliest and most elegant hotels in the Far East. We stayed for almost two weeks while Bill worked on several news items. Then we ran out of money. CBC Toronto had apparently sent less money to the office than the trip would cost, and Bill told me he only realized this fact when he went to pay the hotel bill. I was a bit surprised that he found out so late, but it didn't seem to bother him. During the next few months I realized that Bill had very little interest in money. He always seemed to have enough for what we needed, but I wanted to know just what kind of life we could afford. I once asked him when shopping, "Can I buy a doughnut, or can I afford to buy a car?" He just laughed and said, "Why don't you take over the handling of the money?" I did.

Until we had money wired from Toronto, we couldn't pay the hotel bill, so we had to stay. The early days of working in television were a lot different from today.

Singapore is like a smaller and much cleaner Hong Kong. Lee Kuan Yew, then Singapore's prime minister, was credited for changing the third-world country into a shining first-world city-state in one generation.

Some called his regime dictatorial, but the city sure was clean. Two thousand dollars was the average fine for littering. A cigarette butt or a piece of chewing gum thrown on the street would put you out at least that much—more for repeat offenders, who could also end up with two days in jail. I loved that I could safely wander around, and I managed to write a couple of travel stories that were picked up by three of the Canadian papers. Other than pieces I'd written for the student newspaper, these were my first printed stories, and I was very proud when they were published. I never thought I would do print journalism: although my English was fluent by then, I was used to working in television and writing for the spoken word, where grammar and spelling don't matter that much.

From Singapore we drove first to Malacca, in Malaysia, and then to Kuala Lumpur. On our way to Malacca, we stopped at a small motel. When we opened the door to our room and turned the lights on, the pillow on the bed was black and moving with cockroaches. These weren't flying, but they were bad enough for me to run screaming out the door. It took me almost a year of living in the Far East to get used to seeing cockroaches everywhere.

From Malacca I took a side trip with our driver to see a fortune-teller who I'd been told was famous. He had a small house on the side of a country road. His office was decorated with all types of ceremonial swords and knives. He wore a purple robe and a big smile as he welcomed me to his home, offered me tea, and looked at my hand and the tea leaves.

He then started telling me who he thought I was and recounting things that had supposedly happened to me in my past. When he asked me if he was right, I told him no. Nothing he said was right; he was way off from the truth. He got very angry and picked up a big kris, which was like a military dagger, and chased me out. I ran out to the road, happy to get away and back in the car. He was the worst and certainly the scariest fortune-teller I ever visited—and there have been a few!

Kuala Lumpur back then reminded me of Don Mills, a green suburb of Toronto, or any other well-kept North

American suburb—probably a nice place to live, but not very interesting for a traveler. Bill did a story there, and then we were off to Jakarta.

Jakarta was a huge, sprawling city, and not pretty—crawling with people, cars, bicycles, animals, bicycle rickshaws, and rickshaws powered by people on foot. I was amazed that we could get anywhere.

Because of the upcoming Nixon visit, the Hilton, the only international hotel at that time, was booked solid. After searching for quite a while, we found on the outskirts of the city a motel that had three rooms—two for us and one for the equipment. It was comfortable enough, but the service was somewhat . . . different. Bill needed a suit dry-cleaned for an interview. The next day they brought it back washed. Oh well, they tried.

We were staying only a couple of days in Jakarta, mostly to get our accreditations, which was my responsibility and not an easy one. I had to take all our papers to the media center, which was already set up at the Hilton to handle the presidential visit, and wait for hours to get clearance. Bureaucracy was alive and well in Indonesia, and everything to do with the government was slow going. I also had to do some research and make sure we would have a place to stay during the actual visit. The most interesting part of our first visit to Jakarta was that it was on July 20, the day Neil Armstrong took the first step on the moon. We watched the moon landing on a grainy black-and-white TV.

The next day we flew to Bali. Bill had to be there for the opening of Bali's international airport, and I had to research and shoot a half-hour television program, *The Dance Dramas of Bali*, for my old CBC show, *Take 30*.

I believe Bali to be one of the most beautiful and mystical places in the world. I fell in love with the island, its forests and volcanic mountains, its beautiful rice paddies, the beaches, and most of all, the people.

Bali is a Hindu island with hundreds of temples. Today it is a favorite of tourists from around the world, but when we were there, it was just being discovered. Kuta Beach, now known not only for its beach, but also for its many nightclubs and restaurants, was then deserted. At the entrance of each temple there was a big sign telling women not to enter if menstruating. Nevertheless, the ambience of Bali was magical.

The dance dramas of Bali are so famous that the group I was to film had just returned from a tour of Europe. We were to film them doing some traditional court dances and the kecak, known as the "monkey dance" in English. It is a Hindu ceremonial dance drama based on the story of the Ramayana, one of the major epics of India. It is complicated, beautiful, dramatic, and very long.

Since in my show I was to cover many different dramatic dances and also explain the stories behind them, I had only four minutes in which to show the monkey dance. I was worried and asked to have a chat with the leader of the group.

Talking to this Balinese dancer and choreographer was amazing. I saw him rehearse—he was a great dancer—and after just a few minutes of talking to him, I realized that he was an all-around professional. When I told him I needed a shorter version of the dance but still needed to tell the story, he said no problem. He started to snap his fingers, as all dancers do when thinking of the music, and said, "We'll do thirty-two bars of the intro, sixty-four bars to set the scene," and he went on to break up the story into small pieces. This helped to tell the most important and visually interesting parts of the long, complicated dance drama. We then agreed on the tempo, ran a couple of rehearsals, and filmed a magnificent piece. He and his dancers were awesome.

After reading up on Balinese folk dramas, I knew that our next piece would require us to travel deep into the forest. I shared a car with a young German photographer I'd met at the monkey dance rehearsal. He was doing a travel story and was also interested in seeing the Kris and Fire Dance, which is performed in a trance. It all happens late at night in the dark, lit only by torches.

After a long drum introduction accompanied by humming and the waving and spraying of essences, some of the dancers lay over sharp krises, large military daggers. They stayed there for minutes, then jumped off and continued to dance. There was no blood, they were not hurt, and we could see plainly that no one had held them up on the krises. Trick or magic, we never found out. To me it was magical.

I seriously considered staying in Bali. A lot of people do. The island is enchanting. But after being married for just a month, and with Bill's jam-packed schedule, that wasn't in the cards.

Bill covered the opening of the international airport and we headed back to Jakarta for the Nixon visit.

We were there two days before President Nixon arrived. In preparation for Nixon's visit, I did a lot of research to give Bill for his story, and I checked all timing and contacts to make sure Bill's film would be on the first plane to New York. Canadian TV didn't have the budget to have special planes standing by to get the films back to be processed in New York. CBC had a deal with the American networks to fly their film back to New York and then on to Toronto.

The night before President Nixon was to arrive, I got a phone call from the assignment editor of the *Toronto Telegram*, one of the papers for which I wrote freelance articles. He told me the political writer they were sending to cover the Nixon visit was ill and couldn't make it to Jakarta. He asked me if I would cover the event. I said of course, I would be happy to.

For me, this was a big deal. The Nixon visit was huge; the story would be front-page news. Since I had all the research I had done for Bill's television piece, I was confident I could do a good job. I was excited and told Bill. He said that while it was a compliment to have been asked, there was no way he would allow me to file the story, as it would scoop his own coverage.

I tried to explain that because of the delays with film shipping, print stories always appeared before television stories did. No matter who wrote the stories, print would always appear first. He still said no, and we had a big fight. He was worried that his bosses would see my byline and think the arrangement was wrong, since they were paying for me to be there in the first place. I still truly think they wouldn't have minded.

But I also saw that he had a point: I wouldn't have been in Jakarta to file the Nixon story if CBC hadn't paid for my trip as Bill's assistant. So I had to keep quiet. I agreed not to send in my story until later, but I was furious. This was the first of many times we fought over work. Bill couldn't stand the feeling of being in competition with me. And he didn't tolerate any political opinions from me either, unless they were the same as his own.

After our long swing through Southeast Asia, it was good to get back to Hong Kong. Bill and the crew left for Vietnam soon after, and I settled into a life of luxury.

I made a good friend in Hong Kong, Bob Hathaway, the political attaché at the Canadian embassy. He had lived in Hong Kong for a long time, and he showed me around. He was desperately in love with a gorgeous Canadian woman, Marsha, who taught at the University of Hong Kong, but she wasn't returning his feelings.

The two of us went everywhere—temples, alleyways, racetracks, movies—and my favorite afternoons were when we went to the Chinese cemeteries. Families brought picnics to the graveside of their loved ones and spent joyous afternoons there. When we walked around, we had to be careful not to step on someone's grave, but everybody was friendly and happy.

Bob helped me with my research for a half-hour show I got green-lighted by CBC, called *Living in Hong Kong*. In our research, we visited acupuncturists and other experts on Chinese medicine, as well as historians, cabinetmakers, jewelers, and tailors, and we interviewed "China watchers," as the journalists covering mainland China were called. One of them was Australian magazine writer Richard Hughes, author of the book *Borrowed Place, Borrowed Time: Hong Kong and Its Many Faces*. He had a serious crush on my mom.

I also started taking Cantonese lessons. I have a good ear for languages, and while I had difficulty with the many tones needed to speak Chinese, I enjoyed learning.

Bill's big ambition was to be the first Western television journalist to report on Communist China. For some reason, a few print journalists were allowed into South China at that time, but television crews were not yet allowed. He spent much time getting close to the Chinese diplomatic representatives—we entertained them a lot—and eventually he got the word that he and the crew had been granted an entry visa to Guangzhou (Canton) and Guangdong Province, which is next door to the New Territories, which belonged to Hong Kong.

When we applied for our visas and the Chinese officials found out that a woman was part of the crew, they sent us instructions on how I should dress. No skirts and no bright colors. Brown or black pantsuits were required. I was excited but anxious to go to Communist China, especially during the Cultural Revolution. What we were reading about China at the time was similar to but even worse than what we went through in the early fifties under Stalin and his puppet government in Hungary.

To get from Hong Kong to China at that time, you had to walk across the border that separated the New Territories from mainland China. We took a train to the border and then, carrying our luggage, walked across the border and took another train to the Dong Fang Hotel, in Canton. The Dong Fang was the only hotel where Westerners were allowed to stay.

There were a lot of British businessmen staying in the hotel, as well as diplomats and print journalists from all over the world.

Canton is one of the largest cities in China, with wide streets and thousands of bicycles. Back then everybody dressed in brown or black pajamas, called "Mao suits" by most outsiders. There were huge pictures, posters, and signs, all with pictures of Chairman Mao, and groups of children marching everywhere holding the little red books containing Mao Tse-tung's teachings in the forms of short statements and poems.

At our hotel, a supervisor sat by the window on every floor. The first afternoon I was given permission to walk around the streets near our hotel. After walking about a hundred meters, I looked back and saw a friendly crowd of about a hundred people following me. I realized that being a white woman was an oddity in China. I was a little nervous, but it all seemed harmless.

I saw a store with some framed Mao pictures and other souvenirs and decided to try some shopping. I asked for and then pointed to a framed Mao photo displayed high up on a wall, and a little ivory elephant sitting in a basket.

As the storekeeper took the Mao picture off the display wall, he dropped it and the glass broke. To my amazement, he just wrapped it up with the broken glass, took my money, and, smiling, said thank you.

I walked out of the store and back to the hotel with my broken frame and my now close to two hundred smiling followers. At the hotel, I took Mao out of the frame and tried to get rid of the broken glass. That proved to be impossible. I tried to give it to the floor supervisor. She wouldn't take it.

I tried to sneak onto another floor and leave it in a corner, only to find it back in front of our room. I soon realized that this was part of the big Chinese effort at the time to show foreigners that there was no such thing as theft in China. To prove this, there was a large glassed-in cabinet at the entrance of the large dining room, displaying all the found items: eyeglasses, watches, and even false teeth.

The next day we were taken to a collective, a large farm not far from Canton. There was a committee waiting for us and we were invited for tea. There were many speeches

explaining how the collective worked based on the principles and teachings of Chairman Mao. We drank many toasts
to the chairman. It was very hot at the farm, and the tea was
hot water and some sweetener with several flies swimming
in the pitcher.

During one of the breaks, I wandered into a little shop
on the grounds of the collective. I was looking at the items
locked under glass, mostly little red books, various photos
of revolutionary scenes, more photos of the chairman, and
photos of barefoot doctors. I thought this would be a good
place to try out my pidgin Chinese, so I asked the girl behind
the desk some questions about the items and their costs. I
then went back to our table and listened to more speeches
and had more hot water with flies.

We were scheduled to film around the collective, and
Bill was to interview some of the leaders as well as a barefoot doctor. Just as we were getting ready to leave, our inter-
preter came and pulled Bill and me aside. He was very upset
and asked Bill why he hadn't put on his application that I
spoke Chinese. He said this omission could get us into big
trouble. I kept saying that I could only speak a few words,
mostly enough to ask questions without understanding the
answers. He said that this was a bad mistake.

I apologized and promised I would never try to engage
anyone in a conversation.

Every little thing about us was reported.

I felt more and more anxious every day. I was frightened,
and because of my background and upbringing in a similar dictatorship, I found it hard to listen to the shameless
propaganda they tried to make us and all the other foreigners believe. The propaganda sounded the same as I remembered, and Big Brother was watching us everywhere, just

as he had during Stalinist times in Hungary. The children reciting from Mao's little red book were just like my friends and I were in the pioneer movement back home.

The worst example of this was our visit to a bridge about an hour's drive away. It was a lovely bridge over the Pearl River. There were hundreds of people biking over it, and Red Guards with Mao flags and pictures marching across, chanting and singing. Our translator explained that the peasants of the local collective and the Red Guards built the bridge.

He emphasized that no architects or engineers were used in its construction. The bridge was a proud example that counterrevolutionary, bourgeois engineers and architects were not needed and that the bridge was proof of the power of the people.

This was at the time of the relocation movement, part of the Cultural Revolution, when thousands of professionals and businesspeople were shamed by the Red Guards and called the enemies of the people. They were then transported overnight from the cities into the countryside. When the translator finished telling us how the Red Guards and the peasants built the bridge, I made the mistake of asking him if the engineers and architects relocated to the country from Canton were also used to assist in its construction.

He was embarrassed and told me that only enemies of China would suggest such idea.

I tried not to ask any more questions, but in reality I was really upset. We couldn't even talk openly in our rooms at the hotel because the rooms were bugged. I asked Bill to go for a walk and told him what I thought about the bridge and all the other lies and propaganda we heard during the day. He seemed less bothered by it than I, and while I am sure he didn't believe everything, he seemed very impressed by the ideas of the Cultural Revolution and what we were seeing.

To me that seemed naive. I think a lot of people who grew up in North America and have never experienced living under a dictatorship tend to idolize the ideals of Socialism and the promise of a Communist utopia. Bill and I had another big fight, but I realized that I was in China on his dime, and just as I had to back off in Jakarta, I needed to back off again.

Backing off was getting more and more difficult; I had strong opinions and I also wanted to build an independent career, one that didn't depend on him. I learned a lot traveling with Bill's crew and doing research, but I felt I had to do more on my own.

Visiting China was interesting but very stressful, and being back in Hong Kong was wonderful. As soon as we arrived, we headed to the luxurious Peninsula hotel to have a decadent lunch. It seemed even the Communist Party members living in Hong Kong missed the capitalistic luxuries, since they too were lunching at the Peninsula hotel.

Soon after we returned from China, I got a call from a woman I knew who worked at the *South China Morning Post*, Hong Kong's best English-language newspaper. After the usual pleasantries, she asked me if I had ever done work in PR. I said no but inquired why she was asking. She told me there was a great job opening at the Mandarin hotel. I thanked her and said I would think about it.

Many journalists of the time, including Bill and to some degree myself, held the opinion that doing public relations was selling out and that PR people were just "flacks." Later in my career, as I did public relations for various organizations, governments, and international corporations, I learned to passionately disagree with that opinion.

When thinking about the possible PR job, I realized that perhaps it could help me resolve my problem of not feeling that I had a life of my own.

The Mandarin was, and still is, one of the most elegant hotels in Hong Kong. It sits on the island, facing the harbor on one side and the busy shopping street, Queen's Road Central, on the other. It is luxurious but not opulent. It has oriental flare and colonial sophistication. It is simply beautiful.

I called the Mandarin and got an appointment with Kai Yin Lo, the hotel's PR director. She was a gorgeous woman—educated in the United States, dressed in designer clothes, and wearing spectacular jewelry. We had a short interview.

She seemed pleasant but not very interested in me. To my surprise, after ten minutes she said, "Go and meet Mr. Stafford, the general manager. If he likes you, I am OK with everything."

Mr. Stafford was a handsome, very conservative Englishman in his early forties. We had a good interview, and he asked if I could start the next day. I said I would love to, and I was hired.

The PR office was located on the second floor of the hotel. It was a lovely, comfortable office with two large desks, and it had a small entry room where the secretary worked. Kai Yin and I shared the office.

On my first day, Kai Yin gave me a half-hour summary of the PR department's responsibilities, which included producing a biweekly newsletter and issuing press releases when needed.

The press releases were mostly announcing the arrival of celebrities, information on VIP visitors staying at the hotel, and information on large banquets and events held in the various public rooms and ballrooms. We also handled all media calls and dealt with requests from our celebrity guests.

I told Kai Yin that between the two of us, the workload sounded manageable. She then told me she was leaving for New York and London the next day and would be away for two months. Then, with a big smile, she added that she had an important lunch to attend and that she had all the confidence in the world in me, and she cheerfully left the office.

Now I understood why I was hired so quickly. I was to run the department alone. Nothing like a half-hour training session to prepare you for your first job in PR!

Fortunately, the secretary, Suzy, was staying. She took me around the hotel and showed me the various public rooms, the bars and restaurants, and the many luxurious suites, and introduced me to the department heads. We went over the files, looking at the many past press releases and announcements and the upcoming state and celebrity visits.

Since it was 1970, the year of the Osaka world's fair, there were many. Most visitors to Expo '70 stopped in Hong Kong either on their way to Osaka or on their way home.

Shortly after I started, we welcomed the shah of Iran; Prince Radziwill of Poland and his wife, Lee, Jackie Kennedy's sister; the American singer Sarah Vaughan; Raymond Burr (who played the TV detective Perry Mason); and, to my delight, Prime Minister Pierre Trudeau.

For the shah, our work was limited: we were to take part in the welcoming committee, send out a press release, and arrange media interviews with the appropriate people in his entourage. Princess Lee Radziwill asked me to take her shopping, which was a delight. She was friendly and chatty and bought some lovely jade earrings and some silk blouses. I also shopped with Sarah Vaughan and kept Raymond Burr entertained during a reception. He didn't have a publicist with him, and he offered me a job traveling with him on his publicity tour.

Prime Minister Trudeau was to stay at the hotel for three days. There were many Canadian expats living in Hong Kong, and there was to be a reception for them to meet him. He was also going to tour the harbor in a Chinese junk. I was very excited to meet Trudeau. This was during Trudeaumania, and I was a big fan. I had worked in the CBC control room on election night when he became prime minister, but I had never met him in person.

Three days before his expected arrival, I got a call from the office of Roméo LeBlanc, the prime minister's press secretary at the time. The woman who called told me that they'd heard a Canadian was working in the hotel's PR office, and since they were short a PR coordinator for the Hong Kong visit, she asked if I could take on some of the duties. I was happy to, of course.

It was a thrilling but stressful weekend. After the general manager and all of us department heads welcomed him to the hotel, my big assignment was to be the prime minister's escort at the luncheon given for the Canadians living in Hong Kong. I was to introduce the guests to Mr. Trudeau and, if needed, assist in the flow of conversation—keeping him moving, and making sure there was time to meet everyone. This sounded like great fun, but it was not easy. Mr. Trudeau did not enjoy small talk, most of the guests were a little nervous and somewhat tongue-tied, and I had to make sure there were no long pauses or awkward moments. Since I was also nervous and in awe of our handsome PM, it was not an easy task.

Just before I left work, I was asked by a member of his entourage if I knew a couple of young ladies who would like to show Mr. Trudeau around Hong Kong at night. It was an unusual request, and I declined, saying that I was relatively new to Hong Kong and married, so I didn't know too many single girls who would like the assignment.

Then I got worried. Our handsome bachelor prime minister, known for his charm and pirouettes, was a chick and media magnet. I dreaded the tabloid coverage if he intended to paint the town. I hung around the hotel until 2:00 a.m., hoping to chase the paparazzi away. No success, as the front page of the *Star* and the two other Hong Kong tabloids showed Mr. Trudeau entering the Mandarin at 3:00 a.m. with a gorgeous woman on each arm.

The morning of the PM's departure, as the general manager and I were walking him out of the hotel, the waiting photographers started calling out to him to kiss the pretty lady.

I just kept smiling and walking, and before I knew it, the PM gave me a quick hug and a kiss, then did a pirouette and gave me another kiss, and we ended up on the front page of the Hong Kong papers. I later had the photo framed and now have a signed copy of it in my office. I loved my job at the Mandarin and slowly got to know and truly enjoy Hong Kong.

My mom joined us in Hong Kong, and to my surprise and delight she also loved the city. She settled in quickly. She bought some shiny black amah pajamas and went to a nearby park to do tai chi. We arranged tours to take her to Kowloon and the New Territories, where she met the Gurkhas, Nepali soldiers patrolling the border. We took her sailing and to Macau, where she sat next to the amahs playing the one-armed bandits in the casino for hours. She also taught Asam and five other amahs to make Hungarian stuffed cabbage, which we served at a house party.

We were settled and happy and were trying to have a baby. I had always wanted a little girl, and the time seemed perfect to make it happen. Then Bill got the news that he was to be transferred to London. As much as we liked Hong Kong, we were excited about the move. Bill had another assignment to finish in Vietnam, and then he went to Toronto to finalize the details of his new job, so Mom and I made plans to go ahead and get set up in London. She and Bill got along famously, and Mom had decided to come and live with us there.

Through my hotel connections, I managed to get us on a cargo ship from Hong Kong to Kobe, Japan. In addition to Mom and me, there were seven other passengers on the ship: three couples and a lady in her late eighties. She ate with the captain and was friendly to all of us; we saw her walking three times around the ship every morning. We learned that she was the widow of a ship's captain. She had traveled with him for many years, and he negotiated with the ship's owners that after his death, she could continue to live on board. I later heard that she lived on the ship for another seven years.

From Kobe, we took a taxi to Osaka to board a flight to London. We had to wait a few hours at the airport. In the lounge, a young Japanese chef was making crêpes suzette. Mom, who was a great cook, thought he didn't do it quite right. She politely asked him if she could help, and ended up making crêpes suzette for everyone in the lounge.

It surely was a fun way to say goodbye to our life in the Far East.

Top: Street in Canton, China
Middle: A barefoot doctor in China
Bottom: Bill in Canton

Top: Canadian prime minister
Pierre Elliott Trudeau and me
at the Mandarin hotel

Mom

CHAPTER 9

LONDON

When we arrived in London in the fall of 1970, Mom and I headed for the Inn on the Park hotel. CBC had agreed that we could stay there while looking for an apartment and waiting for Bill to arrive. He was off in Northern Ireland, covering the conflict there.

Mom had never been to London, and I had only been there once before, for a few days, visiting cousins. Living in London was like a dream come true for both of us. When I was a little girl, Mom used to take me to the British embassy in Budapest. We were allowed into the lobby, and she used to show me the picture of the queen. She was very impressed by all things British and explained to me that none of the horrible things that went on in Hungary under both the Nazis and the Communists could ever happen in England.

Other than being impressed by the beauty of the historic city that we had always regarded as the center of the world, it was good to discover that the people were also friendly. The cabbie who drove the big black taxi we took from the airport to the hotel was warm, funny, and welcoming.

We settled into two lovely rooms at the Inn on the Park, a Four Seasons hotel on Park Lane. We visited all the tourist attractions, from the Tower of London to Buckingham Palace to Covent Garden, and so many others.

We visited our cousins: Mom's first cousin, Ica, and her husband and daughter; my second cousin, Anni; and her husband, Péter Frankl, who by then was a famous concert pianist. They all left Hungary for London in '56. They lived in the neighborhood of Golders Green. Anni and Péter had two young kids, Judy and Andrew. Péter was giving concerts around the world, and Anni traveled with him. When they were away, Anni's parents took care of the kids. Mom and I got the chance to hear Péter play one of Tchaikovsky's piano concertos at Royal Festival Hall.

One of my close friends from Budapest was now a principal dancer with the Festival Ballet; Mom and I went to see her perform. We quickly reestablished our childhood friendship, which was wonderful.

Mom and I found a lovely flat on Palace Court, almost across from Kensington Gardens and near the Russian embassy on Moscow Road. The three-bedroom apartment was spacious and bright with a huge balcony. We knew it was perfect, but Bill wanted to see it and the network required his signature before we could sign the lease. Oh well; we ended up living like queens at the Inn on the Park hotel for two months before he could come home and approve the apartment.

I must have been born under a lucky star, because I had great luck when it came to finding a job in London. The InterContinental chain was opening its first hotel in the city. Since the Mandarin, where I had worked in Hong Kong, was also an InterContinental hotel, I managed to get an introductory letter to Peter Balas, the manager of the new InterContinental in London. As it turned out, Peter was a Hungarian American. He hired me as PR manager.

The Portman InterContinental, located on historic Portman Square, was scheduled to open in about six months. I was to start three months before the opening. The timing couldn't have been better. Mom and I had time to furnish our new apartment, learn our way around London, and enjoy the city for a bit. I truly believe that the year and a half we spent in London was one of the best times of our lives.

Life in London was not the same as in Budapest—not quite European—but it was close. Mom found her small grocery shop, her butcher shop, a lady who did alterations, and a shoemaker, and she got to know the neighbors quite well. She soon became friends with Dame Edith Evans, one of the legends of the London theater, who lived on our street.

We missed our dog, Nelson, who couldn't come with us to London from Hong Kong, but he ended up just fine too. Bill's mom and her two retired sisters in Nova Scotia ended up adopting him. Nelson became the apple of their eyes, and he bossed them around for many happy years.

We soon got Muki, a tiny miniature poodle puppy whom we adored. We were busy house-training him when we noticed he had started to wheeze occasionally. Then he suddenly fainted and we thought he was dead. We rushed him to the vet, who diagnosed him with congestive heart disease. He suggested we give him back to the breeder where we had gotten him. But we loved him already and wouldn't dream of it. The vet told us Muki could have surgery, but his chances of surviving it would be fifty-fifty. We asked what would happen if we didn't opt for surgery. The vet said he would live a good life for maybe four years or so. He also told us to give him brandy if he fainted, which we thought was odd. But that is what we chose to do. Muki was a happy dog, and Bill and I were never sure if he really fainted or perhaps became an alcoholic and pretended to faint just to get the brandy. He lived with us for six happy years.

Bill was traveling most of the time, and running the house was Mom's domain. When Bill was home, he enjoyed the city, and because Mom liked cooking and running the house, we entertained a lot. We bought a used Volkswagen Beetle, the old kind without heaters, and I loved to drive around London and the countryside.

I got in touch with my former producers back at CBC and suggested some feature story ideas from the UK. Soon I had the green light to film a twenty-minute documentary segment for *Take 30*, titled "The British Eccentrics." We based the mini-doc on an interview with Hungarian author George Mikes, who'd just written a book called *How to Be an Alien*, which had a chapter on "the British eccentrics."

The highlight of the show for me was filming a suburban family in Eastbourne whose hobby was studying American indigenous life. Once a year, they erected a tepee in their perfect English garden, dressed up in Native American clothes, and invited their next-door neighbors for a music-and-dance performance of traditional North American folklore. It was quite bizarre but perfect for our film, and they were friendly, wonderful people.

A month later, while Bill was on assignment in the Middle East, I arranged to be in Cairo for a few days for a new project. I'd always wanted to go see the pyramids and the Nile. I did some research and suggested a ten-minute-long segment to *Take 30* about the lives of women in Egypt. My producer liked the idea, and I was pleased that I could pay my way, do some interviews, and see the sights. In Cairo, I met Christina, the wife of the cameraman working with Bill. She was originally from Palestine. She was with her husband in Egypt, and we were both surprised to find that we looked like sisters. We became good friends and stayed in touch for many years.

I met and interviewed two very interesting women in Cairo. One was a doctor who headed a group trying to help provide women with access to birth control. The other woman had a PhD in education from the Cairo University in Giza. One of the issues she talked about was the extreme difference between the lives of elite and very poor women, and the inaccessibility of education to girls from poor families.

After our interview, the camera crew and I were filming some visuals around the university campus when a group of construction workers started yelling at us. We didn't understand what they were saying, and we continued working until they started throwing stones at us. Thankfully a security guard appeared quickly and they stopped. The guard told me they were upset because my head wasn't covered.

We spent the rest of the weekend together with Christina and her husband. We went to see the pyramids and took a ride on a camel called Canada Dry (at least that's what her handler told us). Later that night we saw the fabulous light show at the pyramids, and then the four of us went to a club where we watched some belly dancers, and after too many ouzos, Christina and I did some belly dancing of our own. The next day we went sailing on the Nile. It was like a dream.

Life with Bill still felt more like a movie than real life; it was certainly more like an ongoing affair than a marriage. Bill was on the road most of the time. When we lived in Hong Kong, he spent most of his time in Vietnam. While we were living in London, he was in Northern Ireland a lot and also covered stories on the Continent. Whenever my work schedule allowed, I would try to join him for a few days wherever he was, if he wasn't covering wars or riots. We got used to this off-and-on togetherness, and since we were both busy it seemed to work for us. I was relaxing in our relationship and had started to really get to know and trust Bill. Underneath the trench-coated foreign-correspondent image, he was an introvert who had a hard time showing emotions toward those he loved. When his eleven-year-old son from his first marriage visited us in Hong Kong, I saw how Bill tried and failed to talk with him and show him the love I am certain he felt. I wondered how it would be when we finally had a baby.

Back in London we were preparing for the opening of the Portman InterContinental hotel.

Opening a hotel is very similar to opening a theatrical show. In the back of the house, sometimes called the heart of the house, you have the kitchen, housekeeping, security, the back part of the reception area, catering, and administration offices. In the front of the house you have the lobby, the reception and concierge areas, the guest rooms, all the public restaurants, meeting rooms, and the ballroom. The front of the house was ready for the opening; the back of the house was far from it.

The PR office was on the main floor, just off the great lobby of the hotel. I had an assistant named Dawn. She was very mod and smart. Our first job was to write and produce a brochure and then work on events related to the hotel's opening.

InterContinental hotels, then owned by Pan Am, had an opening team working out of their New York headquarters. The team was made up of experts in the different areas of the hotel business: catering, housekeeping, reception, concierge, PR. The Portman had a soft opening with little fanfare—just an announcement and a press release. They left it to word of mouth and those of us in PR to create the buzz.

Dawn and I worked on ideas that would help us publicize our facilities. Because of the location—historic Portman Square, just off the Marble Arch—we tried to weave some history into our stories about the pub and the ballrooms, to give the media a hook that would help them write about us.

I quickly learned that doing PR in London was going to be much more difficult than it was in Hong Kong.

The Mandarin was one of the best hotels in Hong Kong, with celebrities constantly coming and going. My job there was mostly just scheduling and arranging interviews with the press. With the Fleet Street journalists, I knew I would have to work hard to come up with interesting angles to tempt them to visit our hotel and mention it in their paper. We wanted to make the hotel a London hot spot popular with locals as well as out-of-town guests.

My first attempt to interest the media was to install a cimbalom in one of our pubs. The cimbalom is an instrument that traces its origins to the Middle East and the Middle Ages; it makes a sound somewhere between a piano and the harp. It is a special and lovely instrument, well known as an instrument of choice for Hungarian and Romanian Gypsies. I found a well-known cimbalom player in London, and we hired him for the pub. I then had the history of the cimbalom as well as the history of Portman Square and Lord Portman's family lore printed on the grease paper we used to wrap the fish and chips we sold in our pub. We then invited all the journalists we hoped would cover our story. Overall the idea was a success, and it earned some much-needed publicity for the hotel and pub.

Next we produced and presented an event we called the Chimney Sweep Ball. The saying "to light a fire under someone" comes from what chimney sweeps used to do. As a play on the phrase, we hired several dancers dressed like sixteenth-century chimney sweeps to come "light a fire" under the feet of the close to three hundred guests so they would all start to dance. The chimney sweeps appeared out of the fireplaces of our three ballrooms. Most of our guests had to pay for the dinner dance; we also invited many young aristocrats, including descendants of the Portman family and their friends, as well as some up-and-coming local singers, dancers, and celebrities. Dawn had a friend at *Tatler* magazine who helped us with our guest list. The dancers also performed several historical dances, which they then taught to the guests. They did the pavane, the minuet, then the Charleston, and of course, later in the evening, the twist and various disco moves. Our Chimney Sweep Ball was a great success, and my boss loved the publicity we got, including pictures of London's young socialites having a blast in our hotel.

Another event I organized was a 1940s-themed "blackout evening." I did some research at the BBC library and found that during the Blitz, the voice of BBC radio was the announcer Alvar Lidell. He was the British version of Walter Cronkite.

I located Mr. Lidell, and he agreed to be part of an evening in which we would simulate a WW2 blackout evening at the Portman ballroom. We sent out invitations and asked all guests to dress in 1940s-style clothes. I also got hold of a 1940s newsreel showing the news from a day in that era.

The guests arrived, and after a welcome drink, we blacked out the room and Mr. Lidell announced the breaking news. Most people in the audience recognized the famous voice. We then played the film reel, and Mr. Lidell wrapped up the evening. Between his voice, the newsreel, and the costumes, the guests enjoyed the nostalgic atmosphere we managed to create.

The journalists found the evening unusual and we got great coverage, and again my general manager was very happy.

I worked very hard at the hotel, but I also enjoyed the job tremendously. It was like being back in show business, and I was the director of the show.

An interesting guest of the hotel around this time was Dewi Sukarno, widow of Sukarno, the first president of Indonesia. This was shortly after her husband's death, before she became the world-famous socialite, businesswoman, and television personality she is today. She was exquisite looking, with a small, soft voice. She was in London to publicize the book she'd just written. I arranged a news conference for her at the hotel, and after the reporters left, Bill and I and the hotel's general manager and his wife had dinner with her. She was a charmer; one could still see in her the skills of the perfect geisha. She had met President Sukarno in 1962, when she was nineteen, in a Ginza hostess bar. She was an art student and entertainer. The fifty-seven-year-old president was in Tokyo on a state visit.

Right after Dewi left town, Bill's mother and aunt came to visit us from St. Andrews in New Brunswick. They had never been to Europe, and we wanted to show them everything and give them a special time. Bill and Mom did most of the daytime entertaining since I was always busy at the hotel. But I managed to arrange a surprise experience for them that I hoped they would enjoy. At the time of their visit, we had an arts-and-crafts exhibit on the Philippines in our hotel lobby. The display included a colorful jitney bus that I'd managed to borrow for a few hours. The driver and I picked up my mother-in-law, her sister, Bill, and my mom, and took them to see the changing of the guards at Buckingham Palace. We got a front-row spot, and the ladies loved the close-up view of the ceremony.

At Christmas, Mom, Bill, and I went home to Budapest to spend the holidays with my whole family. Since my uncle Geza was a big Communist, Bill insisted we buy him a very capitalist-looking velvet smoking jacket. We took presents for everyone. Bill was always generous, whether he could afford it or not. I was usually the one to watch what we spent, but overseas journalists have great expense accounts, and gifts were things we could claim. The fact that we could take lots of presents to our family back home—luxuries we knew were not available there—made both Mom and me happy.

For New Year's Eve, we rented a big stretch limo to take us up Gellért Hill to have dinner at the Citadel. We all dressed up for the evening in our most elegant clothes, high heels and all. Then the limo got stuck in the snow. We got on a bus. Then the bus got stuck in the snow and we ended up pushing it out. Regardless, it was an outstanding evening, with the Gypsies playing everyone's favorite songs.

Budapest in 1971 was still depressing. The lights were not on at the famous parliament building or on the lovely bridges spanning the Danube. The government was saving on electricity. People were afraid to talk freely; the dictatorship was still in force. Mom and I agreed that we'd made the right choice when we left the country. We talked about what our lives would have been like had we stayed. Mom said she was happy that we left, especially since by now she was able to visit with her family. I was also happy that I chose a life in the West, but after being with my friends and going to the ballet and the theater, I had mixed feelings. The ballet would never have been a possibility for me because of polio, regardless of where I lived, but the world of the theater still had a strong pull. Had I stayed home, I probably would have become an actress—how successful, I couldn't even guess. But I missed Budapest and realized that wherever I ended up in life, I would always have two homelands.

Back in London, the early seventies were exciting times with the fashion—minis, maxis, and hot pants; the Twiggy look; and Vidal Sassoon hair—as well as the music, clubs, and theaters.

Through my work at the hotel, I had access to theater tickets and entry to many clubs. It seemed like we had it all. Bill was successful in his work, although he was often in danger when working in Belfast; I was happy in my work; we were still trying for a baby; and Mom was in her element running our home.

Since I was better with numbers, I always did the household accounts and paid the bills. One day when Bill was in Paris on assignment and I was home, an invoice caught my eye: it was for two return air tickets from London to Paris. Two tickets? I was upset and suspicious; exactly whom was Bill taking to Paris with him?

I was about to call him and ask just that when the phone rang. It was my doctor's office, telling me that I was pregnant.

After more than two years of trying, I was pregnant! Mom and I danced around the apartment. We were both so happy.

Now I had two reasons to call Bill . . .

CHAPTER 10

KATHY

Shortly after I learned that I was pregnant, Bill was transferred back to Toronto. I was sad to leave England. But for Bill, it was a big promotion, and with the baby coming we were eager to find a home back in Canada.

I had a difficult pregnancy and spent a couple of weeks on bed rest in a London clinic. The English doctors were worried about my flying to Canada, but since Bill was transferred, we couldn't possibly stay another six months in London.

We decided that Mom would stay in London and handle the move, and Bill and I would fly to Toronto, rent an apartment, and eventually find a house.

Unfortunately the doctors were justified in their warnings. I had to be taken to a hospital directly from the airport upon arrival to Toronto. They stitched me up to prevent a miscarriage and told me that I would have to spend most of the rest of my pregnancy in bed.

Bill and I rented a two-bedroom apartment on Lawton Boulevard, and a few days later Bill left to go on a cross-Canada trip for CBC. It was a tough time for me. I was alone and had to stay in bed, and Mom was still in London. If it wasn't for two of my close girlfriends, I don't know how I would have managed to stay sane. A month later Mom came back from London, and things got easier. I was feeling better, but not for long.

I was six and a half months pregnant when my water broke. We lived on the seventh floor of the apartment building, and for some reason the elevators were not working. We got downstairs and to the hospital, but it became obvious in the taxi that the baby was coming.

The birth was hard in spite of the baby being early. At that time, nobody was allowed into the delivery room, which didn't go over well with my mom. Knowing her, I wasn't too surprised when a familiar figure bent over me and gave me a kiss. It was Mom, who had snuck a surgical nurse's gown out of a bin in the corridor and slipped into the room in disguise to be with me.

Kathy was born at four in the morning. The doctors showed her to me but took her away immediately. They told Bill that they didn't want us to get close to her because the likelihood of her survival was next to nil. She weighed two pounds six ounces. Today she would have had much better odds, but this was in 1972.

They took me up to a hospital room to rest, but I couldn't rest or sleep. I was terrified Kathy wouldn't make it. I wanted to go see her, but they wouldn't let me until the next morning.

Bill went with Kathy and the doctors across the tunnel to Sick Kids Hospital to register her birth and name. We'd agreed that she would be called Caterina, after Caterina Valente, the singer and dancer, but Bill registered her as Katherine, so that was that.

The next morning they wheeled me over to Sick Kids to see my baby. She was in an incubator, under bright lights. She was smaller than my hand; her skin had a yellow tint, and she had wires sticking out of her everywhere. But she was kicking. The nurses said that was important, as it showed her energy for life.

One of the biggest dangers for preemies is that they often forget to breathe. There were four incubators in the room, and a nurse was going around the incubators, flicking the babies' heels one by one, to remind them to breathe. Kathy spent five weeks in the incubator. During the first two weeks, Mom or I would sit next to her, flicking and touching her little heels to make sure she'd remember to breathe. Thank God, she did. She was growing, and slowly she lost the yellow color to her skin. I practically lived in the hospital, but I could only touch her heel and watch her kicking away in the incubator. While Kathy was still in the hospital, we moved into our new home. We'd bought a three-bedroom bungalow, with a finished apartment in the basement, in a lovely area of Toronto. Mom moved in with us, planning to stay for the first six months to help with the baby, and then move into the condo we had bought in the heart of Rosedale, not far from our house.

Our new home was lovely, but I hardly spent any time in it while Kathy was fighting for her little life. I would wake up very early in the morning to call the hospital to make sure she was still alive. After that I would go sit next to her incubator for most of the day. Bill was also worried, but he spent little time in the hospital. He used to get sick to his stomach seeing Kathy all wired up and yellow. He told me later that while he was worried about her, he was even more worried about me and what I might do should anything bad happen to her. The doctors were reluctant to give me much information on what to expect for Kathy, about her chances for recovery, and about her future. I desperately wanted to know more, and so I figured out a way to get more information to save my sanity. I suggested to CBC that I could do a freelance news story on premature babies and how the doctors at Sick Kids Hospital could miraculously save many of the babies born weighing less than two pounds. Given the green light, I could now interview all the doctors on 7B, the preemie floor, and find out about the risks and predictions for the future development of preemies like Kathy.

Finally, one day while I was sitting next to Kathy's incubator, the nurse took her out, bundled her up, put a little knit cap on her head, and gave her to me.

She also gave me a miniature bottle and said, "Here, feed your daughter."

That was the first time I let out my breath and cried. The worry and anxiety I had tried to keep bottled up for the last month all came out as I practically bathed my little girl in tears.

After that day I was allowed to feed her regularly. I also learned to bathe her in a soup bowl. We took Kathy home when she weighed five pounds. She was very small, but alive and healthy. Mom was there with me, but Kathy was so tiny and we were so worried that we also hired a nurse to help. I am convinced that I loved my little girl even more because I knew what it meant to fear for her life. She was my miracle baby. Mom felt the same way and so did Bill, but he didn't spend very much time with her. He was working hard, and I think he acted the way many men of our generation did at the time, leaving the house and the baby to the women. As the months went by, Kathy started doing well, and she became a sweet little toddler, the joy of my life.

Kathy and I enrolled in a research project run by Sick Kids Hospital to find out at what age otherwise healthy preemies catch up developmentally with babies born at full term. She did very well—in fact, before she was even three, she was better than I was at putting simple puzzles together. We were happy to hear that Kathy would completely catch up by age four.

Mom moved into her new condo when Kathy was just over a year old, and we got a live-in nanny so I could go back to work.

Bill had been named head of TV News at CBC. That meant that I couldn't apply for my old job at the news; it was not allowed. Instead, I managed to get in at CBC's public relations department as producer of the Toronto station's promos.

This was a fun job, especially because the station was switching from Channel 5 to Channel 6 and I got to produce all the promos for the changeover. We had a good budget, and I got permission to use CBC stars, the comedy duo from *The Wayne & Shuster Show*, singer Juliette, and my former TV dance partner from my time teaching ballroom dancing on *Take 30*, Paul Soles. My office in the CBC public relations department was next to a large area for the women that worked the phones for customer service. They answered all questions from the public about the different CBC shows and dealt with complaints. There was a very large clock on the wall in their area, and I used to see most of them glancing at it as it was getting close to five o'clock. At around five minutes to five, they would start picking up their purses and putting away their things, and at five o'clock on the dot, they rushed toward the door. As I watched them, I felt sorry for them and grateful that I'd managed to do work I enjoyed.

Soon after the completion of the promo series, I got a call from my friend and mentor Dodi Robb, who was the first person to give me a chance in television. She had been named head of daytime television, and she'd decided to create a daily half-hour series, produced entirely by women, with each day's show dealing with a different issue.

This was a first for CBC Television. Dodi offered me the Friday slot, which she'd named *TGIF,* and asked me to be the producer covering Toronto's entertainment scene. I jumped on her offer. Even though taking it meant I had to quit my PR job—a solid staff position with security and a pension, while the producer job was a contract—I was very happy to accept.

I was to cohost the show with a wonderful British cartoonist and writer, Ben Wicks, and a young man named Alex Trebek. Yes, that Alex Trebek, who would famously become the host of the wildly popular game show *Jeopardy.* I was sad when he died recently.

Ben and I did the location stories and Alex did the studio interviews. We covered films, theater, clubs, and galleries— everything that was interesting in the entertainment scene.

We taped the show on Thursday nights. After the taping, my script assistant and I would have chicken cordon bleu for dinner across the street from the studio, at the Four Seasons Hotel. We did that every week for two years; it became a tradition. The show aired Fridays at 2:30 p.m. We had a good audience, mostly women, but many men watched it too.

Just before the end of our first season, I had a difficult meeting with Dodi, our executive producer. She told me that she was pleased with the show, but that the program director of English television didn't think people who spoke with accents, other than refined mid-Atlantic accents, should be on-air hosts.

She said in order to keep the show going for another year, we would have to let Ben go, and I would become producer-director but would no longer be an on-air host. I tried to say that this sounded very discriminatory and that Ben was brilliant, Cockney accent or not. As long as we were understood and produced good stories, this was unfair. I was furious. Canada was officially very proud of its multicultural policies and its welcoming of immigrants. There was a lot of messaging encouraging us to become Canadians but keep our distinctive home cultures as well. Multiculturalism was one of Prime Minister Pierre Trudeau's big ideas and was supposed to be more inclusive than the US's "melting pot" approach. Now I realized it was all just talk.

Dodi agreed but said she didn't think it was worth a big fight with the "Kremlin," as we called the building where the executive offices were.

Dodi was my mentor and my boss. There wasn't much I could do.

Ben was going to go to the media and charge the program director with discrimination, but Dodi talked him out of it. The following year I produced and directed *TGIF*. Alex left for Hollywood, Ben left the show, and we hired Doug Lenox as the host. Doug was a great-looking freelance writer and broadcaster—with the perfect accent and a booming voice.

I enjoyed directing the show; it reminded me of my years in the sixties, working in the control room as a script assistant for TV news. Whether a show is live or just live to tape, the control room handles it the same way. There is a tight schedule for all the studios, and there is no time for mistakes. Responsibilities are clearly defined, and the technical producer, or TP, is the boss.

The producer-director controls the content, but the TP controls what makes it to air. This was common knowledge to all of us working in production, but the point was driven home to me one dreary winter night when I was directing the taping of *TGIF*.

The phone rang in the control room. I answered, and it was my mom, saying Kathy was very sick and I should come home right away. I told her we were taping the show, and I couldn't leave. I asked her to call Bill.

She said she'd talked to Bill, but he was in a meeting at a friend's house and told her she should call me. Mom said Kathy had a high fever and we needed to take her to the hospital. Mom didn't drive, so I hung up and told the TP I would have to leave.

He told me I couldn't leave until he got a substitute producer in the control room to take responsibility for the content of the show. If I couldn't wait, he would have to cancel the taping, which would mean no show for the following day. It took close to an hour to get someone to replace me. I was on pins and needles and was calling the shots in a fog. My assistant helped me, but she wasn't allowed to take over; the TP didn't allow it. Finally he got the standby director to replace me so I could leave. I drove home in a snowstorm;

the visibility was next to nil. I was speeding and was so worried and so mad at Bill for not being there that I almost rammed into a parked car. I made it home, and Mom and I took Kathy to the hospital. It turned out she had rubella. She was very ill, but she was fine in a few days.

When I asked Bill where he was, he said he was having important discussions about work and didn't quite understand why I would be upset about him not being available. He knew I directed a show every Thursday night, and he knew the CBC protocol about the director not leaving the studio, but he said he forgot. I could tell that he'd had a few drinks at the meeting, and the episode made me very upset. It forced me to realize that, in his mind, the responsibility for our child was mine alone.

The following year, Bill left CBC to become vice president of news at Canada's newest network, Global TV. This made me very happy, because it meant that I could get a job again at CBC News. I soon did, as a story editor for the public affairs portion of the six o'clock news.

I loved my job. There were three women story editors, including me, and we all worked harder than the guys while making half the money. When we complained, we were told that the men had families to support.

Those were the seventies.

I did some interesting current affairs stories at CBC; several were about abortion rights advocate Dr. Henry Morgentaler and the struggle for abortion rights for Canadian women. I did many stories on health care, multiculturalism, and how minorities vote and participate in politics. I also covered business stories, which I thought were often neglected on our program.

One evening as I was showing one of my edited stories to the show's producer for his approval, he said, "It's good to go, and don't worry about your contract, regardless of what Ross McLean says."

I asked him what the program director had said. The producer told me that Ross talked about not liking to hear foreign accents on air.

This reminded me of the incident when Ben Wicks was fired. My accent by now was very slight, so I lost my cool.

I wrote a news release about how I was discriminated against because I was an immigrant. I suggested that the program director was out of touch with Canada's reality and multicultural policy. I sent it out to all three Toronto daily papers.

The papers covered it, and soon reporters were calling both Ross and me. He denied ever making the remarks and told them that I was constantly on air. He claimed that wouldn't happen if he discriminated against people with accents.

To prove his point, Ross must have given a directive to our show's producers, because for the next six months I was sent on assignments that usually were done by reporters covering the daily news. I was on air practically every day.

Then my contract was up for renewal and I was told it would not be renewed. I didn't have to ask why. My producer just said he was very sorry and hoped I understood that it was not his doing. My colleagues all knew what it was about. But Ross McLean was a dictator at CBC, and none of us had a chance of fighting him.

I was out of a job and upset by the injustice of it. I enjoyed spending more time with Kathy, but I'd always loved my work and derived satisfaction and meaning from it.

It wasn't only my career that had hit a rough spot. My relationship with Bill was becoming very difficult. Now that we were back home in Toronto, with a house and a child, everything had changed. I knew it would, but I didn't anticipate just how much. We could no longer have a marriage that was more like an affair. We could no longer fly around the globe, having weekends together in exotic places. Now we were really married, and Bill seemed to be wrapped up in work, leaving the running of the home and taking care of Kathy totally to me.

In my mind, our marriage read almost like a scenario from a woman's magazine. It seemed to me that I'd married someone who thought he wanted a partner, only to find out that what he really wanted was for me to be his "Adam's rib."

Before we married, we used to enjoy discussing world affairs, and he seemed to listen to my opinions even if they were different from his. However, after I became his wife, it seemed to me that I had to share his opinions or we would fight. I realize that from his perspective, I didn't become the type of wife he wanted, and so he must have been disappointed too. The more I wanted to have my own life inside our marriage, the more he became obsessed with having a "traditional" marriage, where he had a career and I was happy to be his shadow. That was not my vision for my life, and I think we were both unhappy, but regardless, at that time I was determined to keep the marriage intact.

Bill's new job as VP of Global TV kept him busy, and for reasons I found out only later, he didn't want me to accompany him to the many social functions the new television network was holding. When I asked him why, he would turn things around, saying that he'd understood from me that I never wanted to be a corporate wife.

Our house at the time needed some repairs, and Bill didn't want to face the upheaval. Instead he decided to sell our home. I didn't want to sell. I had a gut feeling that a move would be too much for our fragile marriage, and I was afraid of what would happen. Sadly, at that point in our relationship my voice was hardly heard. Like it or not, we were moving into a large apartment in the same condo building where my mom lived—a nice idea, but at that time, it wasn't what I wanted.

Then, just like in a bad movie, one day I was at the hair salon and a former colleague of mine, who was now working for Bill at Global TV, came to say hi. After chatting for a while, she said she was really sorry to see what was happening with Bill and Bodine. She said she found their behavior really disgraceful. Bodine was a gorgeous black reporter, and I'd heard from Bill that he had recently given her a half-hour interview show.

My former colleague must have thought that I knew all about Bodine and Bill, for she went on telling me details and also mentioned having seen Bill at dinners with a very young blonde.

The saying "everything always happens at once" certainly came true for me. I was heartbroken.

While I knew that our marriage wasn't perfect and that I wasn't any "Sugar Plum Fairy," as Bill often said later, I didn't think it was that bad. I confronted Bill, but of course he denied everything. I have never met a man who will admit to cheating unless he's practically caught in the act. After fighting for a week, I took Kathy and moved us into my mom's apartment. Fortunately the renovations in the apartment Bill and I had bought in the same building were almost ready, and we could soon move into it.

This was a tough time. Kathy was only three years old. Bill and I had only been married for six years. I wanted to make sure the rumors about the girlfriends and affairs were true. I followed him by car many nights, and many nights I found out what I really hoped I wouldn't. One morning I took some mail to the coach house where Bill was staying, and as I was walking in, I bumped right into Bodine as she was leaving. She looked at me and smirked.

Then I started dating, hoping to make Bill jealous. It worked, and he and I tried getting back together once again. Our marriage wasn't really over for another four heart-breaking years. We were dating each other and we were both dating others. He was seeing Kathy sometimes, but mostly we were both more interested in our painful games.

The following year Bill told me we had to sell the apartment because he needed his share of the money. So we did. Then Bill decided we needed a house, and so we bought a house together with the idea that we'd give our marriage another try. We planned a family holiday for Christmas at a Club Med in Guadeloupe, but at the last minute Bill couldn't come. He said he had a special assignment at work.

Kathy and I went anyway. Upon our return, Bill told me he just couldn't go through with trying the marriage again. He said there was no one else; he simply didn't feel he could do it. He didn't want to be married.

Many years later, he explained it to me another way: he said, "I was drunk on my own whiskey. I was a VP and a big shot, and I wanted to be free to enjoy it."

I was devastated. I knew that the marriage wasn't working, but somehow I'd thought that Bill would be always there for me. I'd felt that from the first time I met him, and I made a bet on that when, after much soul-searching and pain, I chose to be with him instead of Ferenc, my first husband. But he wasn't there for me anymore, and now I had to face the end of my second marriage. Bill and I divorced the following year.

Having come from a broken family where I missed out on having any kind of relationship with my father, I was hell-bent on making sure the same thing didn't happen to Kathy. I choked down my anger and pride and hounded Bill, who was traveling a lot, to make sure he saw Kathy as often as he possibly could.

During this time I was working on Canada's first network feminist television series, *Some of My Best Friends Are Men.*

It was good to work on the series, to work with other women and on topics that had always been important to me and were even closer to my heart now, because of my personal situation. It helped me find myself again.

Slowly I healed, and because we shared a child, Bill and I became civil to each other. Ever so slowly, we became friends.

Kathy and I settled in a small but comfortable semidetached house near Allenby, a good school that was one of the first in Toronto to offer French immersion. As we were moving in, a lady and her little boy came over to welcome us to the neighborhood. She introduced her son, David, to Kathy. The two kids took to each other and started a friendship that lasted for years. It was a great start to our settling into our new home.

Our house had a nice backyard and three bedrooms: Kathy's room, mine, and a small bedroom we used as a guest room and den. It also had a tiny but closed-in front porch where we had a small stand-up piano, as well as a finished basement apartment—perfect for a nanny. We had our little poodle, Muki, and soon we found a nanny and Kathy started school.

The first day Muki and I walked Kathy to school, Muki suffered from separation anxiety. She ran after Kathy and ended up sneaking into the school. Kathy had to bring her back out, and that made us laugh and feel better. I was so proud and happy to see my little girl starting school. She has forever remained my miracle baby who kicked her way out of the incubator to become my lovely, smart, and beautiful daughter, the center of my life.

We lived in that home for five years. Mom lived in her apartment, which she loved, and we were nicely settled. It was a good time in our lives. We developed a routine: work for me, school for Kathy, and visits with Mom on the weekend. Kathy stayed at Mom's Saturday nights, and I went and visited with them on Sunday for lunch and a swim in the pool at Mom's building. When Bill was not traveling, he would take Kathy for lunch and then I'd get her back Sunday night.

Kathy and Mom were very close, but when my daughter was a child, I sometimes found her hard to read. I had a hard time accepting that, unlike me, Kathy was an introvert. She was obviously very smart; she was a good student, among the best in her class. But communication between us was sometimes difficult. I wanted to hug and kiss her all the time; she would shy away, not liking my emotional behavior.

One night after work, Kathy and her little friend David had big news. They'd decided to get married and wanted to hold a wedding! They were seven years old but very serious. Our nanny at the time was a lovely lady from Jamaica, and she happily volunteered to officiate. The ceremony was held in our living room, with David's parents and Mom and me as witnesses. It was adorable, and the two of them did stay good friends for quite a few years.

Along the way we lost our little Muki. Her heart gradually got worse, and no amount of brandy helped anymore. She passed away at age six, which meant she lived two years longer than the vet predicted when she was a puppy in London. Mom, Kathy, and I were heartbroken, and I decided I didn't want another dog, since the pain of losing one was so great.

I often had to work late, and this caused me many sleepless nights. When I worked late, I missed Kathy's dinner and bath time, and it was the nanny who put her to bed. I also missed many of the mother-daughter activities they held at school. When I did show up to them, I felt so inadequate. One time when we were at school for a family craft hour, I was so bad at crafting that Kathy was embarrassed. I remember she told me that I should have sent our nanny, who was much better at any kind of crafting than I was. I laughed it off, but it hurt. I felt guilty for not being like the other moms at the school, who had more time to be at home with their kids.

A few weeks later we were at a friend's house for dinner and met a couple of musicians and their dog, a black Heinz 57 called Pepi. Kathy and I were all over the little guy, and at the end of the evening the owners asked us if we would keep Pepi for a week. They were going on tour and couldn't take him with them, so they had planned to board him at a kennel. We offered to take him.

Pepi was a black-and-white mutt, one part sausage dog, one part terrier, and one part a million other breeds. He was very smart, funny, and affectionate. After just a few days of staying with us, he could be off leash and would find his way home. When the week was up, the owners called and said they had another engagement; would we keep Pepi another week? I asked them if they were going to travel a lot, and they finally explained that they were hoping that we would fall in love with Pepi and want to adopt him. I understood then that it was all a setup. My friend knew how I loved dogs, and guessed that after a week with Pepi we would be happy to keep him. A few years later, when I started my PR company, Pepi became the Chairman of the Board.

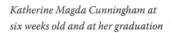

Katherine Magda Cunningham at six weeks old and at her graduation

CHAPTER 11

ANKLE BITERS

Some of My Best Friends Are Men, the show I was working on in the mid-seventies, was a little ahead of its time. One of the program's weekly features was giving an award we called the Shining Porker to a person in the news who'd committed a chauvinistic act. A few months into the series, we gave the Shining Porker award to the pope for coming out strongly against abortion, and the show was cancelled. Our host and we two producers were nominated for an ACTRA Award, but we were all unemployed.

I was on my own with Kathy and still somewhat responsible for my mom. I had to have a job. I applied to various shows, but the only jobs available in television at the time would have required travel, which I didn't want to do.

I'd always loved and been fascinated by real estate, so I decided to enroll in a course to become a sales representative.

I took the course at Ryerson University. It felt like old times, going back to the same school where I'd gotten my journalism degree.

I enjoyed the course and learned a lot that became very useful to me later in life, when I bought and sold my own properties. I was close to finishing when I got a call from my friend Margo, the series producer of our now-bygone show. She was in New York, and she told me she'd found the perfect business for us.

I flew to New York, and she was right.

Her business idea was to open a franchise of the Weist-Barron School of Television. We met Bob Barron and Dwight Weist. Bob was a journalist and PR man and Dwight an actor with a great voice. They had run a successful television school in New York City since 1956. The school had two services: it taught children and adults how to act in television commercials, and it trained executives to make impactful speeches and presentations and do effective media interviews.

They were franchising their business, and so we bought a Weist-Barron franchise for Canada.

I had a little experience in business from running my dancing school, and my friend had a great poker face when talking to banks, but truly we learned on the fly.

We got a line of credit and rented office space, enough for three small studios, and registered as a technical school.

Bob, Dwight, and Lloyd Senger, their director of operations, were flying to Toronto to hold weeklong training sessions for us and our teachers. We recruited five actors interested in part-time work. They included Alex Laurier and Rex Hagon, the well-known hosts of *Polka Dot Door*, a popular television show for children.

The sessions were interesting and practical. We concentrated on the on-camera TV commercial workshops, thinking we would branch out to the corporate world later.

We held an opening reception, inviting the media, casting directors, and theater and TV agents. We gave them a tour of our studios, a short welcome speech and cocktails, and a demonstration of what the school would teach and how.

With my background in publicity—which I had learned mostly in London, where I had to interest Fleet Street journalists in hotel trivia—getting buzz about Canada's first TV school was a piece of cake.

The Weist-Barron method made sense. Applicants were auditioned; then they were given the script for a thirty-second TV commercial to study, and twenty minutes later one of the teachers would take them to a studio. Our studios were equipped with lighting, and camera and playback facilities, as well as props needed in a typical television commercial—in this case a cereal box, a toy, and pots and pans.

Would-be students were asked to practice the commercial they'd been given to study and then deliver it on camera. The performance was videotaped. Then the teacher worked with them for about fifteen minutes. They learned how to do a slate—that is, to professionally say their name and age and the name of the product. They then learned delivery techniques as well as the basics of how to show off the product.

Then they were asked to do the commercial again, and this performance was also videotaped. Both performances were played back to see if there was any improvement and to determine if the student showed potential.

Our TV school's opening was a great success. We were covered in all three Toronto papers and on national TV. We also taped four radio interviews. We put a few small ads in the classified section of the *Toronto Star*: "Want to learn how to act in television commercials? Call us." Our plan was to have six-week-long courses for adults and three-month-long courses for children. The adults would take classes twice a week from 6:00 to 8:00 or 8:00 to 10:00 p.m., and the kids' classes were held on Saturdays. For each class we would hold a graduation, where students would be exposed to the agents and casting directors we invited and sometimes even paid to come.

The school was opened at 10:00 a.m. on a Monday. When I stepped out of the elevator at 9:30, I saw at least forty kids with their parents, sitting on the floor in front of our school's door.

I could hardly make my way through them to open the door. A lot of the kids rushed by me into the studio. It was chaos.

They all wanted to be on TV.

I asked everyone to please find a seat and wait a few minutes for me to get organized.

Soon one of the teachers arrived, and we decided to give out numbers. Before starting the auditions, I made a little speech. I explained that this was a school where we taught acting for television commercials. I explained that we didn't actually put anyone on TV. We would have a graduation to which we would invite agents and casting directors, who might pick our best graduates to work with them. They said they understood.

Our school became very popular very fast. We soon had three studios going every night and all day on Saturday. Our teachers were great. During the six-week courses, students with just a little talent managed to learn how to present TV commercials. They were taught body language, gestures, and eye contact with the camera; voice inflection; and the importance of pauses and transitions. Our graduations became popular with agents and casting directors, and soon we started seeing our graduates in commercials and television shows.

While doing television commercials is not nearly as difficult as acting in the theater or in films, the basics are similar, and many of our school's graduates went on to become well-known actors in Canada, and some went on to work in LA. This was the early eighties. We were happily making money and enjoying what we were doing.

Kathy was growing up so fast; she continued to be close friends with David, and I got to know David's parents quite well. They were a very conservative Jewish couple. Kathy and I spent a lovely Hanukkah evening with them, during which I told them that my mom was Jewish but that I was brought up as a Catholic.

David's parents suggested that since Kathy didn't get any religious education from me, I should see a rabbi to see if she could become Jewish and enjoy the benefits of belonging to a synagogue and community. I didn't know much about Jewish culture, but since I felt inadequate for not having given Kathy any religious tutoring, and I very much wanted her to have the feeling of security that I thought belonging to a religious community would give her, joining a synagogue sounded like an option.

I went to a Reform synagogue and talked to the rabbi. After a half-hour interview, he told me that in order for Kathy to convert, I would first need to do so. After that they would have to make sure that I could provide a religious Jewish environment in our home. I knew I couldn't do that, so that wouldn't work for us.

Not long after that, I thought I found another solution. I enrolled Kathy in the Bishop Strachan School, a private school with a great reputation. It offered courses in world religion. Kathy stayed there till she graduated from grade thirteen in 1991. She later told me that although she did learn about the various world religions, the school was conservative Anglican and she had to go to chapel every day. This turned her off religion of any kind. Still, she got a great education at BSS and made lifelong friends.

Kathy had a once-a-week relationship with her father. I knew that wasn't enough but hoped it gave her some security. I also developed a close relationship with my younger half brother Leslie, who at that time was living in Ottawa. I hardly knew my two half brothers, Leslie and Peter, before Leslie surprised me with a visit to Toronto after he graduated from the University of California, Berkeley. "Less" and Pete are eight and nine years younger than I am, so I only knew them as babies at my father's house before they left Budapest. Then when Mom and I came to Canada in '56, they were living in Rivière-Beaudette, just outside of Montreal. I visited them a couple of times. They were ten and eleven, and they didn't speak Hungarian and I didn't speak English, so we communicated in French. They were true Canadian kids, playing street hockey, and I thought they were very cool. Once when we were in Dad's car, the song "Love Me Tender" came on the radio. I loved it and asked the name of the singer.

They looked at me and said, "You don't know who that is?" I said, "No, but he's good." They told me it was Elvis.

When I asked who Elvis was, they laughed and asked me if I was from the moon.

Leslie came to visit me ten years later, just as I was preparing for my wedding with Bill. He called me from the airport and said he was on his way to Montreal, where he would be starting graduate school in the fall, and he wanted to see us. He was now a handsome and very smart young man. It was wonderful to see him again, even better now that we could both speak English. We became very close and still are. After my divorce from Bill, when Kathy and I were on our own, Leslie was our only family other than Mom.

During the time when I was running the TV school, AIDS hit Toronto. Some of our teachers were gay, and because of the nature of our work, we all moved in the acting and entertainment world, which was especially hard hit by the virus. These were tragic times. Friends and colleagues were sick; many were dying. The community lived in fear.

Around the same time, other TV schools started to pop up. Our school was good, and we never promised anything that we couldn't deliver, but we started to have unfair competition. Soon newspaper ads appeared: "Become a TV star. Call us . . ."

We never guaranteed our students television appearances, so we couldn't compete.

Business slowed to the point where we couldn't make a living. We split up our partnership. Margo kept the school and later opened a talent agency to offer a place for our graduates.

I decided to keep and develop the other service the Weist-Barron franchise offered, presentation skills and media training. I went to New York and took a refresher in

the W-B course, then came back to Toronto to start my next
venture, Media Techniques.

CHAPTER 12

PRESIDENTS TIE THEIR SHOELACES TOO

My Hungarian "reawakening" started after my divorce was final.

It began with the renewal of friendships I had neglected during my six years of marriage and including the years I lived in Hong Kong and London.

One old friend was now a doctor with a chalet in the Blue Mountains, a ski community near Collingwood, Ontario. The lodge there was like a gingerbread house straight out of "Hansel and Gretel," and always full of "56ers," as we refugees of the revolution called ourselves. It was Little Hungary in the Blue Mountains. Learning to ski was a must in that community, and Kathy and I followed suit. She learned very quickly, being nine years old. I, on the other hand, was very scared and wondered how my polio leg, the right one, would work on skis. I hired a private instructor, and we both had a big laugh at my body's reaction the first time I started down from the top of the baby hill.

When the instructor said, "Follow me," my legs automatically opened into a perfect second position, which meant my skis turned out in a straight line and I stood comfortably in the middle but couldn't move an inch. My teacher laughed and said it was a position he hadn't seen before, and he suggested that turning my feet into a snowplow would be a better idea. I never became a good or fast skier, but I managed. Both Kathy and I enjoyed skiing and the many weekends we spent in Little Hungary in the Blue Mountains. There were other kids and teenagers there, and I was happy to see that Kathy was not the only one who didn't speak Hungarian. I still feel bad about not trying harder to have her learn the language, but always working and living in an English-speaking environment made it a challenge.

After launching my new business, I worked on getting a brochure ready so I could start networking and selling the services Media Techniques would offer. The key services were training people in presentation skills and teaching them how to give effective media interviews.

Helping businesspeople learn to give better television interviews was something I had wanted to do since my time as a reporter at CBC. I remember one assignment, when I was interviewing a well-known accountant about a new federal tax law and how it would affect people in various tax brackets. He explained everything to me clearly in our pre-interview, but when we did the actual interview on camera, he gave complicated technical answers. We tried several takes, but he didn't get much better.

Back at the office, we edited the story and found we could use only short clips of him talking. For the rest we used voice-over narration to summarize and clarify what he was saying.

He called me afterward to ask why I'd used so little of what he actually said. I explained why I had to paraphrase and told him that in order to be quoted verbatim, he needed to give concise and short answers. He asked if we could discuss this further at lunch.

Over lunch he asked me if I could give him some practice interview sessions and tried to persuade me to become a consultant, saying there was a real need for what I had to offer. At the time, I wasn't ready. But the time to take his advice had now arrived.

One of my Hungarian friends was George Jonas, a brilliant writer and director. He was the author of the book *Vengeance*, about the 1972 Munich Olympics massacre, which Steven Spielberg later used as the basis for his movie *Munich*. At the time he was married to Barbara Amiel, who became the infamous Baroness Black of Crossharbour.

The power couple had just written the bestselling novel *By Persons Unknown*, about the murder of Christine Demeter in Mississauga. Because of the Hungarian connection, I covered the story for CBC, and the three of us were together a lot, talking about the case. Barbara and I had worked together years before, when she was a script assistant on *Take 30* and I was doing my dance segments every Friday. She was now going on a book tour across Canada to publicize their novel. They both knew of my new business, Media Techniques, and my need to network to get new clients, and Barbara kindly offered to introduce me to the event organizers for the Board of Trade of Ontario and other venues where she spoke.

The Board of Trade held a regular event that included a speaker and a networking session. Thanks to Barbara's intro, I was invited to speak at one of these events.

It was my first promotional presentation.

I gave a speech and did a demonstration about the importance of effective presentation skills, which was a key service of my new business. My intro line was "Many people fear public speaking more than death"—a cliché that for many rings true.

After that opening, I talked about how one could overcome that fear, and I included tips and techniques to help accomplish that. Then I asked for audience participation, inviting someone to come up to the podium and read a short speech I had prepared about the importance of healthy eating and exercise. It was neutral in content and easy to read.

A volunteer came to the podium. I gave him a couple of minutes to read the speech while I talked a bit more about effective presentations.

Then he gave his speech, which I videotaped. After he finished, I gave him some tips—for instance, I suggested that he pause before starting to speak, establish eye contact with a few people in the audience, and read ahead in his text so that it didn't look like he was reading.

We practiced bits of his speech and discussed conversational delivery, learning to end some sentences on an up or down note. I then asked him to do the speech again, and again I videotaped his performance. We played back both videos, before and after. He and everyone else in the audience could see the improvement. He sat down to applause, and I went on to talk about how to give media interviews.

After my presentation there were refreshments, and many people came to speak with me. I was equipped with new business cards with my company name, Media Techniques, embossed on them.

I could hardly believe my luck. The communications directors of GM Canada and Coca-Cola Canada and a manager from Bell Canada gave me their business cards, asking me to call them to discuss some future workshops.

I called each of them the next day. Since power breakfasts were the "in" thing in the early eighties, I invited each for breakfast at the Park Plaza Hotel. I made two breakfast dates and they both went well. However, the man from Bell said he would like to see my office and studio. We made a date for his visit in about ten days.

The problem was, I didn't have an office, never mind a studio. I was working out of the townhouse of a dear friend, who let me use a tiny office in the back corner. After I stopped panicking, I called a Hungarian acquaintance who owned a few office buildings on Merton Street.

I told him my predicament and asked if he had any offices available that I could use for just one day. Luckily, he had just kicked out a company for nonpayment of rent, and he had a furnished suite with three offices standing empty. He said I could use them for a week or so, if I promised that I would rent from him when my business picked up.

I went to see the offices. They were furnished with leather furniture and were large, light, and expensive looking. Perfect!

I moved a camera, a video playback monitor, and a light into one of the offices to make it look like a studio. I arranged for a friend to come in for a half day and play secretary and another friend to work in one of the other offices. It was a good setup.

I invited my mom to come and see "my offices." I sat behind the oversized desk and asked her what she thought. She laughed and said I looked like a business tycoon. Shortly after she left, as I was admiring my office setup, I got a call from the man from Bell. He said, it looked like the day of his visit was going to be very busy, but he didn't want to cancel, so why didn't I go to his office to discuss the workshops? I said of course I would. Looking around, I thought, *At least Mom saw my business tycoon offices!* As it turned out, she was the only one.

I later rented a small space with one office and one studio-office from my acquaintance, also on Merton Street. I made cold calls and had breakfast meetings. Soon I had promises from GM, Coke, Bell, the Ministry of Consumer Affairs, and Shell Canada. It was a great start, but the closest tentative date for the first workshop with Coke was in four months. I needed money in the interim to live on and to cover my office expenses.

I needed a job to support my future business.

I was at the hair salon at Yonge and St. Clair, sitting under the dryer, when I read an article in *Toronto Life* about the $30 million renovation of the historic King Edward Hotel. The story said that when completed, it would be Toronto's first world-class hotel. I could hardly wait for my hair to get done.

From the reception desk at the salon, I called the King Edward and asked who was responsible for the hotel's PR. They told me Argyle Communications. Right from the hairdresser's, I called Ray Argyle. He was in, and I told him that I'd just finished doing PR for the opening of the InterContinental in London, and that before that I was PR director of the Mandarin in Hong Kong. I asked if he would be interested in me helping him with the opening of the King Edward.

I saw Ray that same afternoon, and he hired me to be the PR account manager for the opening.

Working at the King Eddie was a dream. It was Toronto's first luxury hotel, originally opened in 1903. Features like its Crystal Ballroom and Oak Room made it the most fashionable hotel in the city. Elizabeth Taylor and Richard Burton snuck into the hotel before their wedding in 1964.

By the seventies, however, the King Edward had gotten tired and old. It was closed and near bankruptcy when Trusthouses Forte bought it and invested $30 million to bring the grand lady back to life.

Marble was brought in from Italy, crystal chandeliers were installed; it was a huge project. I took Toronto's media, print, and radio and television reporters through the hotel while the work was being done. They all adored the hotel and the story of its rebirth. The opening on May 7, 1981, was an elegant and grand event.

While still working at the King Edward, I was getting ready for my first series of corporate workshops, for the executives of Shell Canada. I'd gotten Shell as a client through one of my cold calls. I used to make my calls early in the morning, before nine o'clock. Very often the communications person I was calling would answer. Later in the day it would always be an assistant or secretary and I would need to leave a message.

When I called Shell, the communications director, John Watkinson, answered. Before joining Shell, he had been the communications director for David Peterson, Ontario's premier in the late seventies. Before that he had been a journalist. He became an important person in my life, both professionally and personally. When he became my client, he referred me to many new clients and introduced me to two of my best friends.

One of them was Lyn Hamilton, the communications manager for Shell. She came down for lunch across the street from the King Eddie, and together we prepared the first communications skills training agenda of my new business. With the Shell workshops, I finally started using my new offices. I hired a few consultants to work with me: radio and television journalists Larry Solway, Bruce Rogers, and Ken Cavanagh.

I began the workshops by asking participants to make a short speech introducing themselves to the group. Bruce Rogers would then do a light informational interview, which we taped and played back to the client to point out strengths and weaknesses.

Next Larry would do a tougher, more confrontational interview to see if clients could still get their message across. We finished the workshops with a simulated scrum, where a number of reporters ask questions at the same time. For this part Ken Cavanagh and I would join in to help our students practice how to give concise, thirty-second answers that could be used as news clips.

Lyn, who quickly became my friend, left her job at Shell and joined the Ontario Women's Directorate as director of communications. She hired us to train the members of the directorate. This was a fascinating assignment. Apart from working on the topics of equal treatment and opportunity for women in all spheres of life, I met some of the smartest women in Canada.

I loved working on that account, and, as it turned out, the women I worked with during that time were instrumental in establishing my company as a solid business. Most of the original members of the Women's Directorate became deputy ministers in the Ontario government, and they all hired us to train their staff.

General Motors was our next big client. I was invited to pitch the vice presidents at a breakfast meeting in the boardroom of the old GM building in Oshawa.

The boardroom was huge: old-fashioned, full of dark wood, elegant, and intimidating. At that time, media training was a new concept. The common preference in corporate Canada was not to talk to the media or to say, "No comment." Few organizations looked at media interviews as an opportunity to tell their side of the story.

Talking to the four Canadian VPs at breakfast, I felt that I wasn't getting through, so I asked if I could do a dummy interview with one of them to demonstrate what I meant.

The VP of sales of GM Canada was a big bear of a man—big voice, big talk, nice guy, but full of himself. A true salesman. He wanted to do the interview. I think he really wanted to show off to the others how well he could do.

I did a very soft interview with him. I asked him about himself and his family, how he got his job. I led him around the rose garden, which is what we called the technique of asking distracting chitchat questions.

The interview was short. When we finished, I asked him and the other VPs how they thought he did. They said he was really good. I asked them, "How many times did he say anything good about GM cars, or GM?" He never mentioned GM at all.

They got my point and I got the account.

I began planning the GM workshops. Less than a month later, both a VP at Foster Advertising and the VP of MacLaren Advertising asked me to lunch. These were the two agencies of record for GM Canada. To my surprise, they both offered to buy Media Techniques. After negotiations, I decided to go with MacLaren.

Later I learned that the GM account was so big and so important that agencies didn't want anybody other than their staff near the clients. No matter how small my group was at the time, no competition would be tolerated; they wanted control.

The day after I signed the contract with MacLaren, I received my first payment. I bought myself a brand-new car: a blue Chevrolet. It was my first new car—and just in time, since Marcsa, my old Ford (not a GM!), was dying.

Doug Murray, head of the GM account for MacLaren, was to be my boss, but our company was to operate as a separate unit—a profit center. Our offices remained on Merton Street.

In addition to holding workshops for GM executives, we started using video news releases for new-car introductions and also began sending visuals of various GM manufacturing plants and workers to the television networks for use as archival footage. One of the most-used visuals we sent out to the TV networks was a short video clip I called "the Dance of the Robots." The fascinating and somewhat graceful way the robots were moving among the cars on the assembly line reminded me of ballet, and I couldn't resist editing their movements to Tchaikovsky's "Waltz of the Flowers" from *The Nutcracker*.

Next we proposed a regular video magazine program to be distributed to all of GM's forty thousand employees. When we got the green light to do a pilot, I again hired Ken Cavanagh to work on the program. We called the show *GM Magazine*. We presented it to the client, and they loved the idea.

GM Magazine had an upbeat, newsy talk show format hosted by Ken. The program covered manufacturing news, sales of the different brands, news from the different plants, and human-interest stories about the employees. It was an informative internal communications program and proved to be a huge and ongoing project.

We produced a fifteen-to-twenty-minute video magazine every two weeks in English and French.

We were responsible for both the production and the distribution. This was before the internet, so we shot and edited a master on high-quality Betacam and distributed on VHS. We rented a large studio in the main floor of the same building of our office, and it became a dedicated video studio and editing facility. We hired two producers and a camera crew, as well as a studio manager and editor.

Now we had an upstairs and a downstairs. Upstairs we did communications workshops; downstairs we did video production.

And I finally could have Pepi, the Chairman of the Board, with me at work full time.

GM Magazine ran for six years. They were busy and wonderful years for Media Techniques. In addition to GM, we also worked for Imperial Oil and Bank of Montreal. We averaged three media-training workshops a week, mostly for the various Ontario government ministries.

By the mid-eighties, I had completed my buyout term with MacLaren. I got my business back, and I was running the show. I loved it.

Around this time I started dating an executive at GM whom I'd met when he was a participant in my media-training workshop. He was a good-looking, smart man who had traveled all over the world, liked theater, and was fun to be with. We'd become good friends before we started dating. He was separated from his wife and lived with his two children: a teenage boy, Mark, and his older sister, Sherri. After a few months we decided to move in together. Looking back, moving in with him and his kids may not have been a great choice, but it was something I guess I needed to do at the time. I felt lonely and I wanted to have a partner again. Kathy had told me many times how much she would have liked to have brothers and sisters. Living with Earle and his kids seemed to be the answer.

Earle and I moved into a lovely big house on Lonsdale Road, close to Kathy's school, with three kids, a dog, a cat, and a bird. It was new for me to have a big family; it was also new to have to rush home from work and cook dinner for five. We didn't have a nanny, since we had two teenagers living with us, but that made my life difficult sometimes when I had to work long hours. We all learned to manage, and Earle and I had some very nice times together. We went sailing on the Mediterranean; we went to New York a lot to see shows we both liked; we went skiing at Whistler. We were both making good money, and we were happy to spend everything we made. I wasn't in love with Earle, but it was comfortable.

Bill used to come to the house to pick up Kathy, and he told me he liked Earle too. Bill started hanging around to talk to Earle after dropping Kathy off on the weekends. In fact, one Sunday when Bill and his then-girlfriend brought Kathy home, Earle invited them for dinner. They accepted and we all had dinner together. It was pleasant, but I thought it a little weird. Kathy seemed to like Earle, although later she told me she didn't. My mom was neutral: she said, "If you are happy, then it's fine." I never wanted to marry him—I saw no reason to—but I was comfortable. Then one night we were out late, and when we got home around 1:00 a.m., the phone rang and I answered. A woman asked to speak to Earle, and he picked up on another extension. I listened in on the conversation and heard the woman crying hysterically, saying she was downstairs in our lobby. I decided to go down with him, and she got hysterical again and told me that Earle had promised to leave me six months before, and that I should know that he loved her and I should let him go.

Earle finally made her leave, but it was obvious that the woman was telling the truth or close to it. Earle tried to deny it, as men tend to do. I told Earle to leave, that it was over. He didn't leave for a couple of weeks, and it was painful, stressful, and awkward. And in spite of the fact that I really didn't love him, the betrayal hurt terribly. I started thinking I was to blame, for why else would guys cheat on me?

Eventually we sold the place we shared and split the money, and I bought a small house on Oswald Crescent. And for some reason that must have made sense at the time, I decided to have a big extension built in the back. I hired a small contractor to do the job. He told me it would take three months to complete, so Kathy, Pepi, and I moved into a friend's apartment. The contractor then disappeared with most of the money budgeted to complete the house. It was late fall; winter was approaching. Kathy and I stayed in our friend's apartment for close to six months, trying to find someone to finish our house. It was a difficult time, but in a way, after living in a large family setting, it was good to be with just Kathy. She was a teenager now, very responsible and a good student, with quite a few good friends, but still an introvert. Our time in the small apartment brought us closer.

Eventually my friend Rene, the mom of Kathy's close friend Erika, introduced me to a contractor I could trust and we ended up with a lovely big house—but I swore I would never again live through a renovation. It was very stressful and very expensive.

And then came the recession.

Car sales went way down, GM announced major layoffs and cutbacks, and *GM Magazine* was cancelled. The recession hit communications departments across the board. Media training and video production were among the first things to go.

We were hit hard, as we had a large overhead. I had twelve people working for me at that time, and gradually I had to lay them all off. I had to sublease some of the office while at the same time trying to drum up new business. Even with all the cutbacks, the business was losing money.

We sold the condo where Mom had lived for seventeen years, and she moved into the downstairs apartment in our house. Kathy was in a wonderful but very expensive private school, where her tuition was covered by the child support I got from Bill. As things always happen at once, Bill lost the job he'd had for more than fifteen years, hosting a national public affairs television show. He stopped paying child support.

We were broke. So broke that one afternoon, Kathy and I went to an ATM to get some money for groceries and nothing came out. All my credit cards were maxed out and we had no cash. I remember trying to put a good face on it for Kathy, who naturally asked where we would get the money for dinner. I borrowed fifty dollars from a girlfriend and more from my younger half brother Leslie the next day. By now Leslie was a tenured professor of sociology at the University of Ottawa, and he was very close to both Kathy and me. He saved us for the moment, but I knew that I had to do something drastic to fix things.

My office was around the corner from the offices of Grey Canada, the Canadian arm of the huge American ad agency Grey. I'd heard that they were acquiring small communications companies to offer their clients a one-stop shopping experience. While I truly didn't like being part of a large ad agency, beggars can't be choosers, so I approached Grey.

The president of Grey Canada was Ev Elting, a New Yorker. He seemed like a charming man. Middle-aged, exquisitely dressed, and quite interested in my company.

We began a series of meetings, and he ended up offering to buy Media Techniques. Against my accountant's advice, I took the deal, which was a good upfront payment but a very low salary, with bonuses paid from the profits I made for Grey. I desperately needed the money he offered up front. It would save our house. The rest, I thought, I'd figure out later.

That Christmas a group of us spent a wonderful week in Puerto Vallarta: Kathy; Mom; my brother, Frank; and Kathy's friend Erika and her mom, Rene. It was a trip I felt I deserved to give myself, as well as Mom and Kathy. I felt guilty for putting them through a lot of hardship—especially Mom, who'd had to move out of the apartment she loved.

Mom was eighty-five at the time, and this would be her last big trip. It was great that she had both Frank and me with her. The hotel swimming pool had a bar in the middle, and she would swim between us to sit at the stool and have a cocktail. The trip was a great success for all of us, including Kathy, who had her best friend there.

The first time I met Erika, she was around fourteen. She'd come to dinner at our place one night after school, and I served a lovely pasta dish. She tasted it and said, "Oh, this is from Sanelli's; my mom buys this often." Sanelli's was an upscale grocery store in Rosedale that sold great ready-to-eat dishes.

I laughed at her charming and outgoing style and said, "I have to meet your mom; we seem to have the same tastes."

Her mom, Rene, a lovely Finnish Canadian woman, was my hero for finding me the contractor who finished our house. She and I became good friends and stayed friends for many years.

Meanwhile back home, Media Techniques had been renamed Gabor Communications, and was now a profit center of Grey Canada.

It was a hard transition. I had to fit into a workplace that was elegant and expensive on the outside and nasty and petty on the inside. Ev Elting turned out to be both ruthless and temperamental. "What did you do for me today?" was his first question at every meeting. When we brought in business, we were stars. When we had a bad month, we were publicly humiliated.

A big contract I won while at Grey was from the federal government, for a video series called *Canada Day by Day*. It was to show immigrants waiting for their visas what Canadian life would be like. My client at the Ministry of Immigration, Refugees and Citizenship was Mandira, an Indian lady and a friend of Deepa Mehta, the well-known Canadian-Indian film director. She told me Deepa was going to get the contract but became unavailable.

While working on that series, I learned a lot about Canada's immigration policies and some of the public's changing views on ethnicity. After Mandira screened one of the episodes, she asked me to cut in some more pictures of immigrant ethnic women. I found some great shots of Eastern European women in babushkas. She called back upset, saying the pictures were not of ethnic women, since they were white. I tried to explain that white people could also be immigrants, but she obviously thought "ethnic" meant only visible minorities. Her attitude upset me. I was an immigrant too—part of another wave of immigrants, yes, but we went through hardships the same as all other newcomers.

One of Grey's big clients was TD Canada Trust. I trained many of their executives, and during a media seminar with six wealth managers, I suggested it would be good public relations if they sponsored a television series about personal finance. I told them we could produce it and buy a weekly time slot on Global TV.

We did a pilot hosted by Bruce Rogers, who worked with me doing media training and was well known for reporting on consumer issues. We called it *MoneySense*. Global liked it and TD was happy.

In order to make the series less like a public relations vehicle for TD and more like a consumer-education program, we also partnered with other companies. Our other sponsors were the Association of Certified Accountants and a large life insurance company.

The show was well received. It ran for two years. However, I hated working for Grey. It was a competitive and toxic atmosphere. Also, it was hard for my small company to make a profit, since the overhead Grey charged me was huge.

During my years at Grey, my life at home had its ups and downs. After graduating from high school with very high grades, Kathy had the choice of enrolling in any one of the best Canadian universities. She wasn't sure what she wanted to do, and to my surprise she ended up going for engineering at McMaster University in Hamilton. McMaster is a large campus, with thirty thousand students, and while I wasn't sure about engineering, I was happy to have Kathy just an hour away from Toronto. She seemed sure and happy, and it was exciting to drive her and help her set up in residence. She was sharing a room with another girl, and Pepi and I visited her there many weekends.

At home it was Mom and me once again. She had her own little apartment downstairs with a nice walkout to the patio and the backyard, but I knew she missed the apartment that was her home for so many years. As winter approached, she surprised me by announcing that she was moving to Florida. I tried to talk her out of it because I was worried about how she would do all on her own. I told her we didn't have much money, we couldn't really afford it, but she said her pension would cover her expenses and she wanted to go. So I helped her find a place. Through a lot of research, we found that renting an unfurnished apartment in a nice, elegant high-rise on the beach was half the price of renting a furnished place in a much inferior neighborhood. So that's what we did. We rented a small bachelor apartment in Hollywood, just south of Fort Lauderdale. It was on the beach and had a lovely view of the ocean and a large swimming pool. Most important, it also had a series of stores, including a grocery store, in the lower lobby. For someone in her eighties without a car, it was the perfect spot. We then went to the huge Rooms To Go furniture store and bought light, Florida-style furniture for very little money, then we went to Target for kitchen and bathroom utensils, and in a couple of days we were ready for Mom to move. My credit cards were maxed out and I was worried sick to leave her, but while I had always loved Mom, I had never admired her more. How brave she was, and perhaps how stubborn as well: to move at age eighty-seven to a new state and a new home, where she didn't know a soul, might have seemed crazy, but to me, it was admirable.

After settling her there, I went home to start my life alone. I didn't like it. I was rudderless and didn't know what to do after work. It took me some time to learn how to live on my own. I learned that when you are on your own, you need to make plans in advance with your friends, whether it is dinner, movie, theater, or drinks. I learned to do that, and I was getting used to it.

Then one weekend, Pepi and I went to visit Kathy and found only her roommate there. She told us Kathy was on her way home to Toronto. When we reunited, Kathy told me she couldn't get into the swing of things at school and had decided to take a gap year. So I had Kathy back once more. She got a job for the rest of the year, with plans to go back to school the next fall, this time to Queen's University at Kingston. During the winter we went to visit Mom a couple of times.

My personal life picked up a little when I bumped into an old acquaintance at the coffee shop next to my office at Grey. He was originally from Switzerland and worked in the hotel business; in fact, he had been my first husband's boss years earlier, at the Inn on the Park hotel. Jean Pierre was tall, dark haired, and beautiful—and the best of his many nice characteristics was that he was a fantastic cook.

We started going out and he cooked almost every night for us and my girlfriends, who I suspect were green with envy of my good-looking chef.

Our friendship lasted a few months, until my life once again took a turn that made it impossible to even think of dating. Mom got sick in Florida. She had a cold that turned into pneumonia. I managed to make arrangements first for her to be taken to the hospital and then, when she was over the worst, to fly her home. She seemed to be better for a few days, but then she got worse and needed to go to the hospital in Toronto.

She was recovering nicely and was soon to be released, when the day before I was to pick her up I got a call saying she had broken her hip. Apparently she'd gotten up in the night to go to the bathroom and fallen. She had to have an operation within two days. Frank and his wife, Lou, flew to Toronto. Mom had the surgery and we prayed. She stayed in the hospital for a few days and then was transferred to a rehab facility at Providence Centre. She slowly started getting better, but then we were told that she would be allowed to stay there only two weeks, and after that she needed to be transferred to a long-term care facility or I would have to sign her out and give them a written statement that I would be responsible for her care. They advised me not to do that, for she needed twenty-four-hour care. But I simply couldn't let them put her in a long-term care facility. I didn't have the money to pay for a private rehab place or to hire nurses to take care of her. I couldn't do anything else but take her home.

By this time Kathy was back at university, so I was alone with Mom, and I was still working for Grey. Through Hungarian friends I got linked up with a wonderful woman who had just arrived in Canada from Yugoslavia with her husband and two kids. I hired her to take care of Mom five days a week so I could go to work. Mom liked her and was getting better, but she still needed help around the clock. We had steps in the house, and she sometimes forgot that she couldn't manage them, and her focus wasn't as sharp as it used to be.

It was very hard for me. I was stressed at work, and at home I was taking care of Mom with no break at night or on the weekends. It was too much. I lasted nine months, and then I knew I had to do something or I would collapse. I decided to quit Grey and sell our house. It wasn't that simple, though; I couldn't just quit, because I had a contract. So I had to hire an employment lawyer, and after a lot of money and a lot more stress, I was out.

So here I was again, starting over, this time with Kathy at twenty and my mom now unable to take care of herself.

This was in 1992, when the Toronto real estate market was at the bottom of its roller-coaster ride. I was desperate to sell, and with the slow market, it was tough.

When there were showings, I got Mom out of bed, dressed her in a pretty dress and scarf, and sat her with a book on the living room sofa. Kathy, who'd come back to Toronto to go to Ryerson University, stood in our lovely backyard under the apple tree with Pepi. I warmed cinnamon in the oven and lit candles for atmosphere.

We finally sold our home at a loss, but it was enough for me to live up to my obligation at Grey. I had a budget of $1,800 a month, and we had to be walking distance to downtown or a subway for Kathy to go to school. We needed three bedrooms, at least, since I was determined to start my business again and work from home.

The only places I could find within our budget were depressing and dark. I knew Kathy would be unhappy there and I would lose my mind trying to build a business and take care of Mom, so I made the decision to let it go. By now Kathy was twenty-one. She would be deliriously happy to have a small bachelor apartment near the campus, and I knew I could get that for her at around $500. Mom would have to go into a nursing home, and through some amazing friends with a lot of contacts, I managed to get her into Baycrest Centre, the best long-term care there was and is in Toronto. Baycrest Centre is part of a geriatric research hospital founded by a huge Jewish foundation and managed by the Ontario government. It was the best I could do, but it broke Mom's heart and it broke mine too. It took many years of psychiatric therapy to help me live with the guilt of what I did to Mom and how I let her down by making her move into Baycrest, but at the time I simply couldn't do anything else.

I found a small apartment in an old house on Woodlawn Avenue in Midtown. It was a renovated rectory split into three apartments. Mine was on the main floor, with a lovely living room, a big, bright, and light kitchen, one bedroom, and a small den.

Grey wouldn't let me use the name Gabor Communications, so I registered AGI Communications, set up an office in the den, and went to work.

The success of *MoneySense* proved to me that it was possible to produce solid educational television programs that were paid for *not* by the networks, but by the sponsors. I decided that the key product of my new company would be producing sponsored television series.

The first project of AGI Communications was *Financial Planning for the Future,* a six-part television series hosted by Bruce Rogers and aired on TVOntario. TD Bank and the other sponsors of *MoneySense* stayed with the show.

TVOntario—Canada's educational network, with high standards and very little money—was the perfect network for my new service, producing sponsored educational TV shows and miniseries. Close to 70 percent of their broadcasting is aimed at schools, as part of the curriculum. The other 30 percent is general public education.

I learned that after producing the Steve Paikin show *The Agenda*, the network had hardly any money left to fulfill the mandate of general public education. I developed a strategy to get sponsors with enough money to allow me to produce high-end shows that TVOntario would be happy to broadcast.

I approached associations like the Canadian Back Institute, the Alzheimer Society of Toronto, and the Association for Plastic Surgeons. I explained the advantages of producing a program for TVOntario that would bring attention to their association and educate the public about their cause.

Since professional associations usually don't have big budgets, I searched out their major donors and supporters, and with the associations' blessings I approached them for sponsorship.

One of my first miniseries was *Back for the Future*. The leading organization in the field at the time was the Canadian Back Institute.

I talked to the doctor who led the institute, telling him about my idea of featuring its work in a television series. He said, "That sounds great, but where would the money come from?" I explained that usually it would come from the broadcaster, but in the time of budget cutbacks, they relied on us, the producers, to find the money as well. I researched and found out that the institute's biggest sponsor was Bayer. The doctor made the introductions, and Bayer became our sponsor.

We shot three half-hour shows hosted by Alan Edwards, a well-known television host. We interviewed the CEO and other doctors, therapists, and nurses; showed visuals of the specialized exercise equipment; and included comments from the patients. We also produced print materials with tips for a healthy back.

The next project was *Face of Beauty*, a one-hour special dealing with the various things men and women will do to look young and beautiful. For this show, I approached a well-known plastic surgeon and proposed doing a feature interview with him on the topic and showing him performing various procedures and surgeries. He understood the publicity value of such a show and was pleased to do it. For the money-finding part, I asked him to introduce me to his contacts at Botox.

Botox then became our sponsor, and we produced an excellent program that was broadcast on both TVOntario and Global TV.

Over the next few years we produced many more health-related programs and even more one-minute public service announcements. One of them was for the drug that helps women who suffer from a condition called "overactive bladder."

In the sixty-second PSA, we visually demonstrated how many times a woman with this condition would have to stop to go to the bathroom on a road trip from Toronto to Niagara Falls. Our budget was low, and in order to save money, instead of hiring a professional actress, I played the part of the woman driving the car and stopping at all the service stations. The voice-over explained how taking the drug featured in the video could help women with overactive bladder. The PSA was well done, and it got a lot of play by the networks.

A few weeks later I got a call from my daughter, who worriedly asked me if I was OK, and why I hadn't told her about my medical issues. Soon after that, I was editing at our post-production studio when my editor quietly turned to me, saying how sorry he was about my "condition" and how he hoped the drug would help.

Everyone thought I really had the condition; they didn't realize I was just acting in the TV spot. I shouldn't have been surprised—I was the one who put the spot on the air—but somehow I didn't think it would get that much attention!

I was doing well with my new company and my financial worries seemed to be over, but I wanted to grow the business, so I continued making cold calls to get new clients.

One morning at 7:30, I called the Insurance Bureau of Canada and asked to speak to the communications director.

When he picked up the phone, I went into my well-rehearsed spiel. He listened and started to laugh.

"Agi, I know your spiel and you already worked for me," he said. "It's John Watkinson; you worked for me at Shell." He invited me to lunch.

That lunch launched the beginning of a twenty-five-year relationship with the insurance bureau and the insurance industry.

CHAPTER 13

THE SECOND
TIME AROUND

Soon thereafter I met John's second-in-command, Mary Lou O'Reilly. She was in her early forties and very attractive—tall, with black hair—and, as I quickly learned, very smart. Prior to working at the Insurance Bureau of Canada she was communications director for Providence Centre, the Catholic hospital and long-term care home. Before that she worked in provincial politics in Halifax and had been a newspaper reporter. She had also written a book.

The first video we worked on together was a simple ten-minute-long summary of the communications department's campaigns and achievements from the previous year. It was easy to work with Mary Lou, and she was open to new ideas. She was, like me, a single mom. She had two sons; the oldest was a few years younger than Kathy. We had a lot in common and got along well.

Mary Lou told me that one of the issues she wanted to focus on in our work together was the fight against insurance fraud. She asked me for some ideas.

I knew that the IBC's advertising and PR agency at the time was very good but conservative. I presented her with ideas that at the time were considered "outside the box": a radio series and a television special. She was excited about them, and we hashed out the details and presented them to her boss, John. Since it was an expensive initiative, Mary Lou also needed to present it to the IBC board of directors.

We called the radio series *Suspense Theatre*. It consisted of ninety-second-long dramatized stories about fraud.

We created a structure for the series: we called it "the doughnut." The dramatized story was the doughnut that surrounded "the hole," an IBC message about the fight against insurance fraud.

The television special, *Scruples (or, What Would You Do?)* was produced as a town hall meeting with an audience and a panel of experts. We played short video vignettes on a giant screen, with actors playing out various scenarios. One showed a woman at an ATM, withdrawing cash. The video shows her selecting sixty dollars, counting the cash, and realizing that she received eighty dollars instead. We then asked the audience what they would do in that situation. Would they pocket the money? Or go into the bank and give it back? A panel discussion about fraudulent behavior followed. *Scruples* was shown on Global TV and syndicated across Canada.

Perhaps our biggest assignment for the IBC was helping the industry's fight against the government takeover of the insurance business in New Brunswick.

We produced close to forty commercials in two languages. It was a tough campaign, and in the end the IBC won the fight. In the meantime, my staff had grown to nine people. The Gabor Group, as we were now called, became the insurance bureau's agency of record; my little company was growing and doing well again. Ken Cavanagh and Larry Solway were back working with me for the IBC and on our media-training workshops.

Larry had a large sailboat at the time and was a great host, inviting many of us to sail with him. He kept his boat at the Toronto Island Marina, and I became a regular on the boat on the weekends. I tan very easily and was a dark shade of bronze that summer. I ran into Bill by chance one day. He asked where I got my tan and I told him about Solway's boat. I told him Larry loved company and I was sure he would welcome Bill on his boat.

Bill showed up the following weekend, and he too became a regular after that. That was strange—and strangely exciting. He never brought anyone with him to the boat, and after he started coming, neither did I.

After one lovely day sailing, he asked me if I was hungry. I said not really, to which he answered, "Well, I've got to eat, and you may as well keep me company." We went for Chinese food, which we both loved.

From then on, our weekend sail and dinner became a routine. We talked about his job, as he was back at CBC, working on a new series idea; I talked about my business and, of course, Kathy. Neither one of us was romantically involved with anybody else at the time, or as Bill put it, we were both "pausing for station identification." We started going to movies together and, more and more often, dinners out.

Neither of us wanted to talk about what was happening between us. I certainly enjoyed the relationship. It was easy and so comfortable. I was happy but also scared. I didn't want to get hurt again, but I believed I still loved him somewhere very deep down, where I had buried that love so it wouldn't hurt. Could I trust Bill this time? Had he changed, and had I changed as well? We had been apart for seventeen years. I was lonely, and I wanted us to continue our dates. I was careful not to push it or discuss it. I was afraid it would end.

One Saturday, Larry decided to take the boat with all of us to Niagara-on-the-Lake, offering a bunk for anyone who wanted to sleep on the boat. I didn't, since Larry's boat was lovely above but below deck resembled a bachelor pad. I replied that I would check in to the motel adjacent to the marina.

As I was leaving, Bill followed me. Larry, whom we'd both known for many years, looked at us with a question mark on his face. Then he said, "Congratulations, you two; I didn't know you were an item again." I laughed and said that I didn't either. Bill just took my hand, and off we went to the motel.

Bill and I went on dating for about six months, and I was ecstatic. I was happier than I ever was when we were together the first time around. Bill had become the person I wished he would have been then. It seemed that he loved me, and this time he also respected me as a person.

Kathy, like many children of divorce, wanted us to get back together, but I'm sure that at twenty-three, she thought it was a bit too late for it to matter much in her life. I could see the question in her mind, like, *Why couldn't you guys do this before?* A few months later, Bill and I decided to live together. We'd give it another try.

We were both renting at the time, and I was eager to get back into real estate. I'd always wanted my own house. I was told this was a characteristic of immigrants: wanting a home, something solid to hold on to.

Bill and I were making good money, but we needed a down payment.

My younger half brother Leslie, who had been a loyal friend to me and a steady and constant figure throughout Kathy's life, was there for me again. He loaned us the money and we bought a small house on Shaftesbury Avenue, in the Summerhill area. We got a wonderful Portuguese water dog that we named Barco, the Portuguese word for boat. We got Barco from a breeder in Delaware.

It was a nine-hour drive home, and Barco—a tiny black-and-white fur ball at six weeks old—was amazing. We stopped a few times for bathroom breaks, and he performed each time. Not one accident. We knew we had an exceptional dog.

We were given a carrier and were told to make sure he would sleep in it. We tried, but I just couldn't do it. Into the bed with us he came, which we knew was a big mistake, but Barco was adorable, playful, and loving, and we let him run our lives. We took him to puppy school; we sent him to a training camp; we were told he was doing well. He came home and he was fine, as long as we were home with him or took him with us wherever we went. Left alone, he'd decide to eat the furniture, and his preference was leather. He suffered from separation anxiety.

When he was around six months old and had eaten several pairs of Bill's Italian leather shoes and our leather couch, we finally had to physically stop him. I found a huge dog cage, big enough for three dogs so he was comfortable and could see out. I am sure it was more painful for us than him, and he complained for a few days, but he got used to it and after a couple of months he was fine.

I loved Barco. I was seriously looking into opening a doggie day care so I could spend every day with him. By then Barco was around sixty pounds and stood as tall as my waist. I knew that he was a baby at heart and playful, but if you didn't know him, he could scare you. We were together almost all the time, and he was very protective of me. We spent hours in a nearby park, which was on top of a reservoir; I called it the top of our world. We went swimming in the lake a lot, and he would swim ahead of me and then circle back to see if I was OK.

Our townhouse on Shaftesbury Avenue had a front garden as well as a backyard. The house was close to a ravine, and there were many raccoons around, so we had to be very careful with the garbage. We also built a picket fence with a small gate around our front yard to have a space for Barco to play.

One day when I was taking the garbage out, Barco slipped out through the gate and scratched a woman walking by. I ran out, got Barco in the house, and tended to the woman, offering to check and see if the scratch had gone through her jeans or broken the skin. I asked her to come into the house, I offered to buy her a new pair of jeans, I offered to show her Barco's immunization certificate, but she said no problem, she wasn't hurt, and she left, accompanied by a young man she introduced as her nephew.

I was worried. A dog like Barco, looking fearsome, could be muzzled or put to sleep far too easily. But I didn't hear anything more, so I relaxed.

A week later we were hosting a dinner party when our front-door bell rang at around ten o'clock. My friend Charles opened the door, and there was the woman. I asked her how we could help. She said that when she went home, she found a scratch that was bleeding, so she went to a doctor who told her she may have rabies and she needed to report the incident to animal control. She'd come to tell me that she had done that and someone would be coming to see Barco. I tried to say that Barco had had all his shots and that she had told me she never felt anything on her skin, but she simply said she had changed her mind. Then she left.

The following week an inspector came to our house. Barco behaved and was very nice, but the inspector gave my baby a muzzle order. My seven-month-old Barco was supposed to be muzzled for the rest of his life, unless I could prove the woman who accused him wrong. I was determined to do just that. As a journalist I knew how to research, and after some work I found a dog psychiatrist in New York. I called her and explained the situation. I told her my dog wasn't vicious, just overprotective of me, and I asked if she could help. She said the only way she could help was if she came to Toronto and we could simulate the situation and the moment the "crime" happened. She could find out from Barco's reaction whether Barco was truly vicious or just protective. She charged $200 an hour, but for Barco I would do anything.

She came two weeks later and acted out the scene, and Barco passed. The psychiatrist explained that a vicious dog would have gone after the person he thought was attacking his human. Barco instead went for food, and somehow his disloyalty to me proved that he was innocent. The psychiatrist wrote a lengthy, detailed report. Two weeks later I got a trial date for the case at a small courtroom in Old City Hall. There was a notary public as judge, and a court reporter and a bailiff there. The woman accusing Barco had apparently moved to Vancouver, but she sent a detailed letter accusing Barco of biting her. The judge asked me to tell our side of the story. He then said that after reading the psychiatrist's report, he had written to the accuser, asking her to send the court her ripped jeans as proof that Barco's teeth went through them. She answered that they were old jeans and she had thrown them out. We won, and Barco lived twelve more years muzzle free.

After a year of living together, Bill wanted to get married. I didn't see any reason for it. We had already been married once, and we had Kathy. *Why do it again?* I thought. I was also worried that marriage would ruin the relationship we had. Bill was adamant, saying he never lived with anyone unless he was married. I realized that he was serious, and Kathy was all excited, and so we got married. Again.

Kathy was the host of our wonderful wedding, which took place with mostly the same guests who were invited to our first wedding twenty-five years before.

Because it was an unlikely story and because both of us and most of our guests were in the media, our wedding became a bit of a celebrity event, covered by all the papers. When Bill and I gave our thank-you speech, I told our friends that this second time around, we thought it would be easier to live up to our wedding wows.

Our relationship in our second marriage was very different from the first one. Thankfully, the stress of competition was gone. We were now on the same team. We loved and respected each other.

I believe that the change had a lot to do with the fact that we were now on a level playing field. This time Bill had a good job in TV and I had a successful business, versus the first time, when he was the big-shot head of CBC TV News and I was a young immigrant carving out a career for myself.

We soon fell into a new routine. Bill traveled for his show for four months of the year. If I could, I would join him in a few faraway locations, but mostly I stayed in Toronto, building my business. While this arrangement wouldn't have worked in our first marriage, it worked for us both the second time around.

The offices of The Gabor Group were in Midtown, on the second floor of a townhouse a block away from where I lived. We had grown from two employees to eight, and grown out of our office space. I tried to rent an extra office, but the landlord would only rent us the whole floor, which would have doubled our rent. I figured that if I had to pay that high a monthly rent, I might as well buy a small building and pay a mortgage.

Real estate, here I came again! I started looking around and made two offers but lost both to a higher bidder. Then one day, when I was driving on Yorkville Avenue, I saw a sign on a building under construction: "Business Condos for Sale." I stopped the car, got the phone number, and called the agent, who arrived within ten minutes. He showed me the space. I had the option of buying a seventeen-hundred-square-foot space in the front, overlooking Yorkville, or a smaller unit in the back with a charming courtyard. I decided to roll the dice and buy the bigger unit.

Seventeen Yorkville was a picturesque three-story town-house across from the old historic Yorkville library and the fire hall. A lawyer had converted the building into condo-miniums. There were five units in all.

The basement and ground floor were commercial con-dos, the second floor had two office spaces, and the third floor had a large apartment for residential use. The second floor was perfect for my business.

We had space for three offices with windows in the front, mine being in the middle with a floor-to-ceiling bay window. The unit also provided a large open space for three good-sized workspaces, an editing suite, and two more offices in the back opening to a courtyard terrace.

We moved in three months later and stayed for the next eighteen years.

A hair salon owner bought the back office on the second floor. All of us in the office became her clients. She was good, and her salon was lovely. Once when she was doing my hair, I told her that if she ever wanted to sell her space, to please speak to me first. A year later she did, and I bought her unit. She needed cash, so she was happy with the deal and kept running the salon from there, but now she was paying me rent, which I used to pay the mortgage.

With that purchase, the whole second floor was mine. For many of those eighteen years, sixteen of us worked there, eleven humans and five dogs: Schnitzel, my lovely mini-labradoodle; Snickers the schnoodle; Kathy's dog; Ringo, the bulldog belonging to my wonderful young manager, Ken; and, for a while, Tegan the Chihuahua. One year we pro-duced a video series for social media called *The Real Dogs of Yorkville*. It was fun to work in our office with some great young people. Most of them stayed with the company for

many years, starting with Ken Clarke, whom I hired while
he was in film school. He finished school while working
at Gabor and stayed for twenty years, eventually as COO.
It truly was like a big family, working and enjoying life
together. When we won a contract, we would go to a food
truck, get Italian sausages, and sit on the curb in front of the
skyscrapers to celebrate. We threw elaborate parties for our
clients, with varying themes—from *Mad Men* to Bollywood
and Hungarian folk. I loved the company and "my kids."
They kept me current and we turned out some really good
work together.

An interesting project we worked on came about with
the approach of Y2K: many people believed that the systems
would not interpret the "00" in the year 2000 correctly and
that everything in the computer world would collapse. This,
of course, had major implications for the insurance industry.
Gabor's assignment was to coordinate research and communications with all stakeholders, creating training and
information manuals and producing television commercials
to inform the general public.

The process and implementation of the Y2K "fixes"
proved to be a huge buildup. The year 2000 arrived, the
computers kept working, nothing happened, and we still got
paid!

The millennium brought many new developments to
our lives. We bought a cottage that we named Casa Barco.
Having a cottage had been my dream for many years. Casa
Barco, on beautiful Gloucester Pool, was only a two-hour
drive from Toronto.

Kathy got married in 2001 to a smart young man who
worked in insurance. By this time, she was working in
advertising, for Ogilvy. With Kathy happily married, along

with Bill and Barco—my best four-legged friend—I too was happy. Almost.

Mom was still living at Baycrest Centre and hated it. I'd never forgiven myself for putting her there.

I had my excuses—I had to work, and there was no other option—but I still blame myself to this day for letting her down. I did everything in my power to improve her life. There was a garden center at Baycrest, and I went there with her twice a week. There was also an art shop where we went twice a week. But soon she began asking me why she should do all these things when she never was a gardener and never really liked drawing or painting.

She had a point. So I took her out for dinners and took her home for weekends. For a while she buried herself in reading. But soon she couldn't focus. So she switched to watching television, but after a few months she got tired of that too.

Mom increasingly needed more care, so I hired a companion to take her out when I couldn't be there. But then she suffered a small stroke. She developed dementia, which gradually worsened over time.

Within two years of moving into Baycrest, she was completely bedridden and not lucid.

I started spending every afternoon with her, as the nurse was there in the mornings. Mom loved sweets. Since she couldn't chew anymore, her favorite treats were vanilla custard and ice cream. I used to mix some sedatives into her custard, allowing her to sleep away most of her days peacefully.

Then she had another stroke, which affected her ability to swallow. Each time we fed her, she suffered and came to close to choking with every bite.

I simply couldn't watch. Mom often asked me not to let her suffer, asked me to give her sleeping pills to end her life if she was very ill. It eventually came to that, but I knew that actually fulfilling her wishes would be against the law.

We were both suffering, she physically and I emotionally, because I couldn't help her. Mom and I had always been a team. She was my true partner in life, and I was letting her down.

The doctors wanted to insert a feeding tube to keep her going. I had power of attorney through her living will, and it allowed me to say no to the tube. I went further, ordering the doctors to stop giving her water. This meant that she would die within two or three days, instead of ten days to two weeks.

That decision was horribly difficult, because I wasn't sure if I was making it for her or for me; I just couldn't stand watching her suffer. She was thirsty, and I sat there, letting her lick ice from my hand for hours.

One afternoon I just knew she was going to die.

I went home and got a few of my own sedatives and some vodka. Back at Baycrest, after the nurses finished rounds, I crawled into bed with Mom, took a pill, had a stiff drink, and took her in my arms. Sometime after I fell asleep, her breathing woke me. It became short and quick, then stopped and started again, and then it sounded like a long snore. I had heard about this breathing, and knowing this was the end, I held her tight until the breathing stopped.

We stayed there until the morning, until her body became cold and the doctor forced me to let her go. She was ninety-four.

THE GLOBE AND MAIL *

1998 · PAGE A24

LIVES LIVED

MAGDALENA (MAGDA) KLEIN LACZKO

Refugee. Born in Nagyatad, Hungary, in April 8, 1904; died after a series of strokes in Toronto on Oct. 30, 1998, aged 94.

When I first met Magda — some 30 years ago — she was busy teaching six Chinese *amahs* how to make Hungarian stuffed cabbage. It was in Hong Kong, at the home of Bill Cunningham, a CBC correspondent and Magda's son-in-law. We became friends, and the more I learned about her extraordinary life the more I admired her tenacious will to survive. Her life encompassed almost all of the 20th century and was played out against the great conflicts that swept across the Earth. Those conflicts shaped her life.

Magda was born in a small Hungarian town where her grandfather was a rabbi. When she was 10, in 1914, the Austro-Hungarian Empire went to war. Before she was out of her teens, Hungary had been invaded by Serb, Romanian and Czech armies; it attained its independence and a Communist government had briefly taken power, only to be driven out by the nationalist forces.

Magda married when she was 20, to Ferenc Laczko, from a family of landholders in Transylvania. To marry him, she had to renounce Judaism and convert to Catholicism. It was not a decision easily taken, and it created great conflict within her family.

Mr. Laczko had an import-export business and in the twenties and early thirties they travelled together, to Vienna, Berlin, Rome, Venice. By the mid-thirties, he was a wealthy man. They lived in Budapest and had two children, Ferenc junior, and Agota.

Then Magda's life began to fall apart. She and Ferenc broke up. The virulent anti-Semitism of the Nazis spread like a plague across much of Europe, and Hungary was not immune. As a divorcée, Magda was once again considered a Jew. Some 40 members of her family, including her parents, were killed in Auschwitz. Magda went into hiding in Budapest with her daughter, using false papers, her courage and her wits to survive.

Magda Laczko in 1966 at the Eglinton Theatre.

After the war, she opened a small cafe in Pest, but it was almost immediately nationalized. Two agents of the new Stalinist government walked in one day, and told Magda to get her handbag and get out. During the Communist regime in the fifties, she endured persecution once more, this time because she was considered a member of the old bourgeoisie.

Then, in 1956, young people battled the invading Soviet troops, waiting in vain for Western intervention. With thousands of other Hungarians, Magda locked her apartment and, armed only with salami and some papers, headed for Austria.

She settled with her daughter in Montreal. Her son had come to Canada in 1949 with his father.) Her first job was making feathered hats in a factory. Her daughter, a dancer of some of the world's finest ballet training, decided she could make a living as a dancer in the nightclubs of Quebec. Mother and daughter became a team, with their first performance in Rouyn. Magda played piano, Agota danced — it was a big number, a minuet by Boccherini. The hard-bitten miners of Rouyn must have scratched their heads. Magda and Agota soon developed more contemporary routines.

When Magda's daughter married Bill Cunningham, she moved with them to Hong Kong, then London. In Hong Kong she was up at 6 a.m. every day, dosing tai chi. In London, she and Muki, her poodle, roamed the parks. It was one of the happiest periods of her life.

Back in Canada, in Toronto, she sold popcorn at the Eglinton Theatre, but started to slow down. Her bones became brittle and she broke her hip. Finally, her life was restricted to trying out nursing homes, which became almost a search for identity. She lived in Providence Villa for a time, a reminder of her Catholic husband. Then Rekai House, the Hungarian home. And then, for five years, in a return to her Jewish roots, she lived at Baycrest Centre.

Magda was a survivor, with an impressive appetite for experience. She taught everyone she touched to cling fiercely to life.

Tom Gould

Tom Gould is the former head of CTV News and a long-time friend of Magda Laczko.

CHAPTER 14

BACK TO THE BARRE

I couldn't get used to life without Mom. She wasn't just my mother, she was my life partner, my anchor who had faith in me and convinced me that I could do anything I wanted, that anything was possible for me if I really tried. And now she was gone. Even though she had been ill and not fully herself for a long time, even though I wasn't sure if she heard or understood me, I could still hug her physically and talk to her.

Now I just wanted to sleep and not think. I took sleeping pills because I wanted to rest, to escape, to dull my brain. I wanted to be alone. When I had to be with people, I felt as if I were trying to talk to them from inside a cave. I was surprised that people didn't see the cave walls around me.

My voice sounded to me as if it had an echo, yet nobody else noticed.

I took Barco to our cottage on the lake. It was late fall. I cried and shouted at Mom to come and talk to me. Then I heard a noise outside; I got scared and told Barco to go out into the dark. My vicious, sixty-pound baby refused, so we both went out. We walked down to the black water, but Mom didn't come. Nobody was there.

I went south to Saint Lucia, thinking the sun and swimming, which I love, would help me. The first night they put me in a lovely villa, but I had a panic attack and had to move to be closer to other people. At the resort I met a woman from the Isle of Wight. She was alone too, and her mother had also passed away not long before. We took long walks and talked to one another, and it helped some.

Somehow seeing other guests having fun and enjoying their youth and happiness was comforting. I knew I had to start on the long road to learning how to navigate my life without Magda, my mom.

First I needed to go home to Budapest. My aunts, Mom's sisters Klara and Kati, still lived there. When I went back to Budapest in 1998, they were living together in a two-bedroom apartment. They were old and frail but excited and happy to see me, and it helped to be with them and to be able to go back in time and talk with them about Mom. They also started talking about themselves and how they survived in the concentration camps during World War II, which prior to then they had never, ever spoken about.

Before the war, when they weren't touring Europe as dancers, Klara and Kati lived with their parents in Erzsébet, a suburb of Budapest. Mom and I were visiting the day in 1944 when the Germans marched through the streets. I can still hear the thunderous noise their steps made; I can still see Klara's frightened face and my Nana telling her that it would be all right.

It was never again all right for them. Within weeks, their part of town was named a ghetto and they were not allowed to leave. Within a month they were forced into a so-called collection camp, and days after that they were in a cattle car heading to Auschwitz.

Klara told me when they were lined up for the selection process, my grandfather told her to lie about Nana's age, hoping she would not be sent to the gas chambers. She also said her mother tried to run to her, but a guard hit her and she fell. That was the last time she saw her mother.

Both my grandparents, my Nana and Tata, were murdered in Auschwitz. Klara and Kati talked about some of the horrors they went through. I had read about Auschwitz and seen the horrors in documentary films, but hearing about it from my aunts firsthand was heartbreaking.

Klara and Kati managed to escape. Klara told me she thought it happened after they were walking near a table where SS officers were lunching on roast chicken. One of them, seeing the skeleton-like girls, threw a chicken leg on the ground for them to pick up. Klara, who spoke fluent German, looked at the chicken leg and then said to the young SS officer, "We may look like animals, and you may treat us like animals, but we are not animals," and she kicked the chicken leg. She and Kati could have been shot for that, but instead the young officer followed them and quietly told Klara that he would leave a small part of the wired fence open to allow them to escape. He told them to do it that night. This was a few days before the infamous death march, when the SS made the prisoners walk from one camp to another so that the liberating Russian and Allied forces would not find them alive in the camps. Kati and Klara somehow managed to get back to Budapest.

I remember playing in the courtyard of our apartment building in Pest, when two strangers asked us kids where Magda, my mom, lived. I told them she lived on the fourth floor but was not home. Then I told them Magda was my mother, and that's when they started to cry. They said they were my aunts. They looked like walking skeletons, and I was afraid of them. We talked about this, finally, when I visited Budapest after my mother's death.

My brother, Frank, who by then lived in Dallas, met me in Budapest on that visit in 1998, and for the next three years we both visited our aunts every six months. Those visits were precious for all four of us. Klara and Kati loved seeing us, and my brother and I could relive our childhood as we went to the amusement park and rode our favorite old wooden roller coaster. We also went to theaters and saw performances at my old haunt, the opera. These times in Budapest gave me a chance to see my former school friends, the ballet rats, now retired.

Klara died in 2001. I flew to Budapest on September 14, three days after 9/11, to arrange and be there for her funeral. Two years later I spent the last week of my darling aunt Kati's life with her in Budapest.

Amidst this difficult time there was also joy. In 2002, my grandson, Carter, was born. I became a grandmother and entered a new phase of life. How I adored my little grandson. I spent as much time with him as I could. At age three, he was so smart that he learned the words to all my favorite songs in both English and Hungarian. I loved listening to him sing "Chattanooga Choo Choo."

When Kathy got pregnant again, I told my girlfriend that I was afraid I wouldn't be able to love a second child as much as I loved Carter. Then came Lexi, my granddaughter, and I fell in love again. I became her playmate—and servant! I learned to bake cupcakes. I learned to use the Rainbow Loom. We danced and sang together, we put on shows, we had fun. I was still working, but not nearly as hard as when Kathy was small, and I now had the luxury of time to enjoy my grandkids' childhoods. I love them and continue to spoil them as much as I am allowed.

In 2006, we bought a winter home in Boca Raton, Florida, where we spent Christmases and March breaks. Bill bought a forty-foot Tiara, which we named *Magdalena* after my mom. We sailed on the Intercoastal Waterway to Fort Lauderdale, Miami, the Keys, and Key West, and to Bimini and West End in the Bahamas. The boat became Bill's passion, and we spent some great times on it with family and lots of friends.

Summer weekends were spent at Casa Barco, our wonderful cottage on Gloucester Pool, just two hours north of Toronto in Ontario's beloved cottage country.

One problem at the cottage was the weeds. I declared war on them. Sometimes on visits I weeded all day, and Carter was my master weeder sidekick. At age three he helped me weed for hours, and I loved every minute of being with him.

But Carter and I were no match for the weeds of the lake. We needed help. First we brought about ten wheelbarrows full of sand to the beach part of our property and dumped it in. That helped a little, but only for the few feet in the shallow end. Then we hired a weed-harvesting machine to cut the weeds. It left a huge mess, which took days to clean. The following year I found a Hungarian guy near Barrie who had a chemical solution; it worked great one year, but the next year it didn't.

Next we got a huge carpet that would be secured to the bottom of the lake between the ends of our dock and the swim platform. Laying that carpet became a fun and complicated weekend operation. We were joined by Kathy's best friends, Tania and Mike, and we all walked and stomped on the carpet so it would stay down. Eventually we secured it and it worked well, but only for that area. The last effort in the weed war was procuring a long, knife-like mechanical arm that moved back and forth, cutting the weeds, but we were scared that it would also cut our legs, so we got rid of it. Through all that, Carter and I kept weeding, with little Lexi joining us at times.

When Lexi got bigger, she and I became water buddies. I used to swim with her on my back, and we would play in the lake and the hot tub for hours. As the years passed, both kids became great swimmers; Carter joined the swim team. Lexi grew up to look exactly like Kathy. Her personality is more like mine, though, and we became best friends.

My friend and colleague Lyn Hamilton left communications to become the director of the Cultural Programs branch of the Ministry of Culture for Ontario and then went on to become the director of public affairs for the Canadian Opera Company. She retired and at age fifty became a mystery writer. The series of eleven books she wrote was called the Lara McLintoch Archaeological Mysteries.

Her protagonist owns an antique store in Yorkville with her ex-husband. In the books, Lara gets caught up in murder investigations that invariably take place in a faraway country where there is a fight over a very expensive, very old antique that she bought for their store. Lara eventually has to fly to the scene of the crime, solve the case, and somehow ship the antique back to Toronto. Lyn was a great researcher and a good writer and loved to travel. I thought the mystery series was perfect for her.

When she was planning to write a mystery that took place in Hungary, she asked me to go with her to help with translation, show her around, and be her companion.

"Happy to be asked and happy to go," I said, and two months later we were off to Hungary.

In this particular installment in the series, Lara needed to authenticate the bust of a woman carved from mammoth ivory during the Upper Paleolithic Period, millions of years ago. While researching the book, Lyn learned of a V-shaped cave in the Bükk Mountains region of Hungary that had been the site of items excavated in the 1930s. Lyn decided that perhaps it could have been the original home of the fictional sculpture. My job was to figure out the best way to drive into the Bükk Mountains, and then how to get to the cave.

We made the trip in October, when the leaves were turning. As the sun shone through the golden-yellow leaves, it looked mythical and otherworldly. We stayed in a little B and B, then took a train to the caves.

For me, caves are caves. They were cold and wet. Lyn stayed in there for hours, until she was satisfied that the site would work for her book. We also had a great time antiquing through my hometown. She knew more about antique shops in Budapest than any Hungarian expert, and she felt her book would be better if she visited them all. We did.

We also spent great evenings together. We had seven nights in Budapest, and we bought nine sets of tickets for theaters, concerts, and operas—meaning we sometimes went to shows twice a day. We saw two operas, two ballets, two concerts, and two plays, and finally, as we were packing to get on our flight home to Canada the next morning, we decided we would skip the last show and just have a glass of wine and enjoy looking back on the great trip we had.

Not long after I came back from Hungary with Lyn, Bill and I discovered cruising. We first tried it in the Caribbean with Holland America, on a ship that carried around twenty-five hundred passengers. We liked it, but when we found Silversea Cruises, with smaller ships carrying around three hundred passengers, we became regulars.

One of our first trips was to the Baltics. We started in Copenhagen, went through Tallinn to Saint Petersburg, then on to Helsinki, and ended in Stockholm. We went with my longtime friends Brigitte and her husband, and my best friend, Mary Lou. In Saint Petersburg we went to the Mariinsky Theatre and saw the famed Mariinsky Ballet; to me it was like heaven. We also had a full day at the Hermitage Museum, which was unforgettable.

We also took several cruises in the Mediterranean. One special trip was from Venice to the Adriatic coast, all the way to the Bay of Kotor, also known as the Boka, in south-western Montenegro. Here we saw Sveti Stefan, now a luxury resort on a small island south of the town of Budva. The place was special to me because Mom told me she and my father had their honeymoon there in 1925.

Another one of our cruises stopped in the French port city of Sète. The ship *Exodus*, carrying forty-five hundred Jewish immigrants, had sailed from there to Palestine in 1947. I went kayaking with a group through the city's many canals. We also went to Rio de Janeiro, saw the Christ the Redeemer statue on the Corcovado mountain, and dipped our feet into the ocean on Ipanema beach. We stayed in the wonderful city of Buenos Aires for a week, going to tango halls, one of the many opera houses, and the Pampas.

I worked from the many cruises via the internet, as I now had a staff of ten and the wonders of Wi-Fi allowed me to work while traveling. We were on a cruise in the Mediterranean when I got an email from developers who were interested in buying my office condo on Yorkville Avenue. They wanted to buy all five condos in our building, to build a skyscraper. Three days later another group of developers sent us an offer.

I was handling an auction from a small ship; it was very stressful but exciting. Negotiations went on for days, but before we reached land I had managed to close the biggest real estate deal of my life.

All was wonderful again in my roller-coaster life when my legs started getting weaker. I'd gone through life with one leg weaker than the other; I was aware of my limitations and had learned to compensate for them.

I worked hard to keep in good shape. My legs had started to get weaker once before, when I was sixty. At that time, I started a vigorous exercise routine and succeeded in getting my strength back once again.

But this was different.

I tried to put it down to aging, and once again I started fighting it. When the weakness became more serious in my right leg, the one more affected by my childhood polio, I rushed to my doctor to get more information.

Information was scarce on post-polio syndrome, which is what I have.

For around 25 percent of survivors, post-polio syndrome starts to set in about forty years after recovery from the original illness. It is not known why this happens. The prevailing theory is that when some of the muscles were destroyed by the virus, other muscles connected to the same nerves took over the work. When aging starts to degrade those over-worked muscles, weakness and other symptoms can arise.

Physiotherapy helps those muscles get strong, but since they are doing extra work substituting for the muscles lost to the virus, over the years they get tired and weak. The syndrome was only identified in recent years, and few doctors are familiar with it. So far there is no cure; there is only exercise to slow down the process.

This was terrible news, and I was heartbroken. How can life be so cruel that after surviving and overcoming polio once, you have to live with it again, for as long as you live? Not an easy verdict to accept. While the syndrome is progressive, fortunately the process is slow; one must try to slow it further.

The March of Dimes, the organization founded for the purpose of polio research, has practical advice: "Don't over-exercise because you may kill off your tired muscles, but exercise you must, or the muscles will atrophy." Use it or lose it, as they say.

I've often heard that most polio survivors have type A personalities—or perhaps one needs to have a type A personality to survive polio in the first place. In any case, for an A personality, moderation is very difficult. It also goes against the "no pain, no gain" method that got us walking the first time.

I figured the answer for me was to go back to the barre.

The gym in our apartment building has a long ballet barre, and just like I used to as a child, I established a routine to start my days at the barre. I would listen to music from the famous ballet classes held by the Bolshoi and the

Royal Ballet, now available on the internet, and the music would take me back in time to when I could really dance. Sometimes I would listen to *Swan Lake* or *Coppélia*, and while I was doing simple leg lifts, in my mind's eye I could see the steps of my favorite pas de deux.

In the gym I met a Hungarian trainer, Michael Fekete; I started working with him and we became friends. Michael was a national kayak champion in Hungary and now has a business training kayakers and canoeists, organizing races, and selling kayaks. He first introduced me to the outrigger canoe. I bought one, took it up to Casa Barco, and started my water life. During the summers I paddled most days for hours; I even took part in the Canoe for Cancer marathon held at our lake, Gloucester Pool. I was determined to fight my weak legs and slow down the process.

I also kept traveling. I took my grandkids, Kathy, and her husband to Hungary. It was wonderful to show them my other home. We walked all over my beautiful Budapest, up to the castle, to Margit Island, and to the Palatinus swimming complex, which is still fantastic and fun, in spite of my horrible memories of contracting the dreaded polio-virus there.

I showed the kids the amusement park and the zoo and the apartment building where I grew up, and we all rode the Little Subway. We drove all over my wonderful city, having a great time laughing at the way Google Maps navigation pronounced the Hungarian street names.

We then drove to Lake Balaton, the so-called Hungarian Sea. I spent many of my childhood summers there, and it was great to see my grandkids enjoy it as much as I did. We stayed in Siófok, a popular vacation place on the shallow side of the lake. The Balaton has warm, shallow water; you can walk five hundred meters out and the water will still be only up to your knees. One windy afternoon, Lexi and I spent an hour jumping the waves, just like my friends and I used to do nearly sixty years before.

The village of Nádasdladány and Nádasy Castle, the ancestral home of my first husband, Ferenc, was only a half-hour drive from the Balaton, and on a rainy afternoon we decided to go and see it. I had heard that Ferenc had gotten a grant from the government to restore the family castle and had plans to turn it into an art school and lecture hall, but I didn't know what happened to those plans after he passed away.

As we drove from the village through a lovely large English garden to the castle, we could hardly believe our eyes. The Tudor-style castle was straight out of a fairy tale, an imposing feat of design with a dry moat surrounding its walls. Seeing the imposing castle, Kathy's husband jokingly asked me, "Agi, are you sure you made the right choice when you left this guy?"

The building was built in the thirteenth century, then rebuilt in the sixteenth century and again in 1873 by Ferenc's great-grandfather. The castle is now a museum with large frescos in the Great Hall, a beautiful library, and various salons and dining rooms furnished in the style of the times. There was also a small room where some of my ex-husband's personal items and his portrait were displayed. Ferenc was the last male member of a thousand-year-old dynasty.

We walked around taking pictures of the garden and the castle. After we asked a tourist to take a family picture of us, Kathy turned to me, saying, "Mom, this feels weird. If you had stayed married to him, I wouldn't exist." I told her she would still be mine.

Soon after the castle visit, we drove back to Budapest. We spent our last night in an outdoor restaurant on the banks of the Danube, listening to Gypsy music. I danced the Hungarian folk dance, the czardas, with my adorable granddaughter.

As we have for many winters now, Bill and I spent the winter of 2020 in Florida. Kathy, Carter, Lexi, and some friends joined us for March break, and we all went to Disney World in Orlando. The coronavirus was starting to become news around that time, but the seriousness of it hadn't yet sunk in.

Then Prime Minister Trudeau ordered Canadians to come home immediately, so we did. We self-isolated for two weeks and then started the weird version of Covid life that took up the remainder of 2020 and the beginning of 2021.

It is hard for me to explain how I feel about this virus. I am so tired of fighting the poliovirus that I'm almost in denial that this new virus could kill me. That said, I obey the rules. I wear a mask. I am careful but refuse to allow it to ruin what is left of my life. I was also hugely relieved when Bill and I got vaccinated in early 2021.

In the meantime, I thank God for summer. I am so glad to have Casa Barco, our happy place, where it is almost possible to pretend there is an end to Covid-19.

At Casa Barco I have slowly accumulated a small fleet. We now have two kayaks, a rowboat, two outriggers, a canoe, and four paddleboards.

Besides the joy I get from being in the water and feeling like I am on top of the water, paddleboarding is the best exercise there is for my legs and my balance. The constant movement of the water forces me to keep my knees bent, which is the absolute best workout for my weak quadriceps as I balance against the waves. Getting up to standing position is tricky for me. The first time each summer when I take my paddleboard out, I am petrified of not being able to stand up, but so far, so good.

Post-polio syndrome and I are at war. I know it will win in the end, but I am putting up a really good fight. I know I can't stop the progressive weakening of my muscles; I feel my hamstrings getting overextended, making walking difficult and painful. But I am doing everything in my power to slow down the process.

During the second lockdown due to the coronavirus, in January 2021, my business slowed almost to a standstill. I seriously considered closing shop once and for all. But after a couple of days, just thinking about retiring made me depressed.

I needed to work, and during the pandemic, the only way to get new work was to do it virtually. I had to come up with something new; I worried that I was too old to compete with hundreds or thousands of twenty-year-olds.

Then I thought of my brother, Frank, who went to law school at age seventy-two. When he told me, I said, "But you will be seventy-five when you finish!" His answer to me was, "True, but I'll be seventy-five anyway." *Well*, I thought, *if he can do that, I can do digital.*

I knew from the many times I reinvented myself before that you can only break into new areas of work by doing something that you are really good at, something you really know, and using that as an entry point to something new.

The first time I got into television, I had the unique idea of teaching the camera and the audience how to dance. It was successful because I really know how to teach dancing.

The first time I sold a TV documentary to CBC, it was about Hungary and the lives of young Hungarians. It was successful because I really knew the topic.

I started my communications business by doing media training, because I learned the technique in New York, from the best. Nobody else did what I did at that time in Canada, and I really knew how to do it.

Thinking about all that, the idea came to me:

I have been teaching communications skills in my workshops for close to forty years. Why not go digital with that? Why not teach the same skills virtually, online and through Zoom workshops, as well as through a handbook?

I decided to do just that and more. I wrote a book titled *Public Speaking; Presentations; Media Interviews; Helping You Succeed.* I published the book on Amazon, linked to it on my LinkedIn page and my company's website, and recorded my tips on video and offered them as free downloads. I told visitors that they could get more information by buying my book.

And so I reinvented myself, yet again. It came as no surprise to those who know me well. In spite of my age, I know that I'm not yet done. Creating work that I can enjoy is my strength.

Mom used to tell me, *"Agota, ne ugraj."* The verbatim translation is "stop jumping around." What she really meant was "think before you act." My best friend, Mary Lou, tells me being impulsive is both my best and my worst characteristic. She and my mom are both right. But sometimes if you don't jump at opportunities fast, you may not jump at them at all. That's when you really miss out.

I believe in taking chances and taking risks. Sometimes you win and sometimes you lose. But it is necessary to take chances in life.

When I look back, I have no regrets about the paths I chose. What hurt was when I found my access to a chosen path blocked by circumstances beyond my control. Being stopped just before I reached the finish line. For instance, couldn't polio have come after I got to dance *Swan Lake*? Maybe just once?

But looking back at my life, I realize that the virus made me more resilient and more of a risk taker and allowed me to have amazing adventures. I had to create new dreams; I had to reinvent myself. Along the way I reached higher and dreamed bigger than I ever would have without surviving polio.

As our world seems to be winning the fight against Covid-19, I feel my old hope seeping back. If we can hug each other; go to the theater, the opera, and the ballet; and perhaps travel again, maybe I can beat my poliovirus too.

What I am sure of is that I will keep on fighting. Staying "on pointe" forever.

Our second wedding. My brother Leslie, Kathy, Bill, me, and Brian Nolan (best man).

Kathy and me

The Shaftesbury Times

Bill and me on a cruise stop in Monte Carlo

My aunts Klara and Kati and me at their home

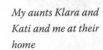

My brother, Frank, and me at the Budapest Opera House

My grandson, Carter

Barco

My granddaughter, Lexi

The Baltic voyage, our best cruise vacation, with Brigitte, Doug, Ed Van Kan, and Mary Lou

ACKNOWLEDGMENTS

I hope you enjoyed reading the story of my life as much as I enjoyed living and writing it.

I want to thank my mom, for instilling in me that I can try anything, and thank my friends, who thought my story should be told.

When I wrote the first few chapters, I sent it to two writer friends. They both thought that I had "found my voice." Christine and Mary Lou, thank you for your encouragement.

Thank you, Anna Porter, for pointing out that my fight with the poliovirus should be a major thread throughout the book. It helped the story so very much.

I want to thank my lucky star to have found my incredible editor, Shannon O'Neill. The manuscript I sent her was 42,000 words. After I followed her comments and suggestions, the edited version was 64,400 words.

Since you're probably reading this after you read the book, you know by now that I worked in television. A basic rule of writing for television or film is that you don't describe in the script what the visuals show. If you write about the heavy traffic on a street where a red truck is blocking the way, you let the viewer see the red truck blocking the traffic and simply write that there was heavy traffic. You don't describe what people look like, how they feel, and what the scenery around them looks like. The visuals will do that.

Shannon prompted me to fill in the visuals, feelings, and times and places with words.

I loved working with you, Shannon. Thank you.

One more big thanks to my daughter, Kathy, for helping me pick and organize the photographs, and a big thanks to my husband, Bill, for his insights, especially on how to best build up to the ending of the book.

And finally, I couldn't have gone through this process of writing and publishing this book without my friend and colleague Martha Dilazzaro, who helped and supported me through the details and decisions. Thanks, Martha.

ABOUT THE AUTHOR

Agota Gabor grew up in Budapest, Hungary, and attended the ballet school of the Hungarian State Opera House. After fleeing Budapest with her mother during the Hungarian Revolution, Agota settled in Canada, where she became a dancer in Montreal. During the 1960s and '70s, Agota worked in television production, eventually going back to school to receive a degree in journalism from Ryerson University. After traveling the world as a freelance reporter and becoming a mother, she founded The Gabor Group, a media company specializing in public awareness campaigns, digital communication, and video production. In 2020, she wrote a handbook on communications and media interviews. *Forever on Pointe* is her debut memoir.

9 781777 904036